MW00415594

STILL LIFE WITH IRIS

A Play in Two Acts
by
STEVEN DIETZ

Dramatic Publishing
Woodstock, Illinois • London, England • Melbourne, Australia

*** NOTICE ***

IMPORTANT BILLING AND CREDIT REQUIREMENTS

For Linda Hartzell

PRODUCTION HISTORY

STILL LIFE WITH IRIS was commissioned and premiered by the Seattle Children's Theatre (Linda Hartzell, Artistic Director; Tom Pechar, Managing Director) in Seattle, Wash., on September 19, 1997. The production was directed by Linda Hartzell; set design by Robert Gardiner; lighting design by RJ Conn; costume design by Scott Gray; sound design by Steven M. Klein; the dramaturg was Deborah Lynn Frockt; and the stage manager was Kara L. Mullen. The cast was as follows:

Iris . . . . JULYANA SOELISTYO
Mom/Miss Overlook. SUE GUTHRIE
Mister Matternot/others . . . . JOHN ABRAMSON
Leaf Monitor/Annabel Lee . . . . ALLISON GREGORY
Mozart/others . . . . JEFF CUMMINGS
Memory Mender/others . . . . DAVID SCULLY
Elmer/Grotto Good/others . . . . WILLIAM SALYERS
Hazel/Gretta Good/others . . . . LESLIE LAW
Flower Painter/others . . . . STEFFAN SOULE

This production featured the Image Influenced Illusions of Steffan Soule and Cooper Edens.

STILL LIFE WITH IRIS (in this published version) was subsequently produced by Childsplay, Inc. [Tempe, Ariz.] (David Saar, Artistic Director; Gary Bacal, Managing Director), in Tucson/Phoenix, Ariz., on March 14, 1998. The production was directed by David Saar; scenic design by Scott Weldin; costume design by Karen Ledger; lighting design by Rick Paulsen; sound design by Brian Jerome Peterson; magic design by Steffan Soule; and the stage manager was Marie Krueger-Jones. The cast was as follows:

Iris . . . . KATIE McFADZEN
Mom/Miss Overlook. . . . . KRISTEN DRATHMAN
Mister Matternot/others . . . . JERE LUISI
Leaf Monitor/Annabel Lee . . . . DEBRA K. STEVENS
Mozart/others . . . . JEFF GOODMAN
Memory Mender/others . . . . DWAYNE HARTFORD
Elmer/Grotto Good . . . . D. SCOTT WITHERS
Hazel/Gretta Good . . . . CATHY DRESBACH
Flower Painter/others . . . . DAVID JONES

This production was mounted in association with the Arizona Theatre Company (David Ira Goldstein, Artistic Director; Jessica L. Andrews, Managing Director) and with the support of the Flinn Foundation.

STILL LIFE WITH IRIS

A Full-length Play
For 4 Women, 5 Men

CHARACTERS
(Pairings indicate actor doubling)

IRIS

MOM
MISS OVERLOOK

MAN/MISTER MATTERNOT
THUNDER BOTTLER TWO
DAD

LEAF MONITOR
ANNABEL LEE

THUNDER BOTTLER ONE
MOZART

MEMORY MENDER
RAIN MAKER
MISTER OTHERGUY
RAY

ELMER
HIS MOST EXCELLENT, GROTTO GOOD
THIRD STRING

HAZEL
HER MOST EXCELLENT, GRETTA GOOD
CAPTAIN ALSO

FLOWER PAINTER
BOLT BENDER
MISTER HIMTOO

Approximate running time: 100 minutes

And she forgot the stars, the moon, and sun,
And she forgot the blue above the trees,
And she forgot the dells where waters run,
And she forgot the chilly autumn breeze.

John Keats

ACT ONE

SCENE: *The MUSIC of Mozart fills the theatre as the audience arrives. MUSIC BUILDS as the theatre darkens, and then plays under as a shaft of LIGHT rises on a tall sign. The sign reads: "WELCOME TO NOCTURNO." Attached to the sign are arrows pointing in various directions. Written on the arrows are the following destinations: "Cloud Factory," "Bird Assembly," "Plant Plant," "Rain Storage," "Fruit Coloring," "Fish School—swimming classes nightly." Standing beneath the sign—his back to us—is a MAN in dark, somber attire. He wears dark gloves on his hands at all times. Unlike the residents of Nocturno, he is not wearing a PastCoat. He stands, reading the sign, as IRIS enters. She looks at the MAN'S back for a moment, then speaks to him.*

IRIS. Are you curious or lost?

MAN. Pardon me? (*When he turns, we see that he wears a weathered sort of tool belt around his waist, containing numerous objects of practical need. The MAN himself has an oddly sinister bearing.*)

IRIS. It's better to be curious than lost, don't you think? Which are you?

MAN. I'm new.

IRIS. Yes, I know. I can tell by your coat. Why have you come?

9

MAN. I'm looking for someone.

IRIS. Well, at this time of night, everyone's at work.

MAN. Doing what?

IRIS. You name it. Whatever you see in the world by day, it's made here by night. Like that fly on your nose— (*The MAN swats the unseen bug away.*) That fly was assembled right here in Nocturno. We crank those out by the millions and teach every one of them to fly. Plus: no two are the same. Our Bug Sculptors are very proud of that.

MAN (*catching on*). Just like snowflakes, then—no two alike?

IRIS. Actually—and this is privileged information—the snowflakes are made in *pairs*. But we separate them and load them into clouds bound for different locations. Don't spread that around.

MAN. I won't.

IRIS. So, you've never been here before?

MAN. Not that I remember.

IRIS. Oh, you'd remember. Unless you've got a tear in your coat. Who are you looking for?

(*LIGHTS EXPAND to reveal the Land of Nocturno, as HAZEL and ELMER—siblings, similar in age to Iris— rush on. HAZEL carries a large burlap sack which is marked: "Spots." ELMER carries a wooden box.*)

HAZEL. I know you took them.

ELMER. I didn't take them.

HAZEL. Where did you put them?

ELMER. I didn't take them.

HAZEL. I bet you're hiding them.

ELMER. I DIDN'T TAKE THEM. Tell her, Iris—

IRIS. What is it, Elmer?

HAZEL *(before ELMER can answer)*. We're almost done with our chores—all that's left is to put the spots on the Ladybugs— *(ELMER removes two large Ladybugs from the box. They're each bright orange and about the size of a cantaloupe. They are without spots.)*

ELMER. But why do Ladybugs need spots, anyway? I think they look fine without them.

HAZEL. And I reach into the Spot Sack and it's filled with these— *(HAZEL reaches into the sack and pulls out several long, black stripes—like those found on a zebra.)*

IRIS. Stripes.

ELMER. There must have been a mix-up.

HAZEL. We can't put stripes on the Ladybugs.

ELMER. Why not? And then we'll put the spots on the zebras.

HAZEL *(to IRIS)*. You're lucky you don't have a brother. It's like this all the time.

ELMER. Can you help us, Iris? No one can find things like you can.

IRIS. I'll help you as soon as I— *(She turns to the MAN.)*

MAN *(interrupts her)*. Your name is Iris.

IRIS. Yes. Why?

(The FLOWER PAINTER enters. He wears a beret and has a palette and brushes on a strap over his shoulder. He goes directly to ELMER, HAZEL and IRIS as, at the same instant, the MEMORY MENDER enters, opposite, pushing a cart inscribed "Memory Mender" in large letters. The cart holds large spools of thread, extra-large buttons, scissors, etc. His hat looks like a thimble. He is

a cranky but caring man, adamant about his work. Upon their entrance, the MAN turns and leaves.)

MEMORY MENDER *(calls out across the distance)*. You there, sir—let me take a look at that coat! Sir, did you hear me? *(But the MAN is gone. The MEMORY MENDER remains at a distance, busying himself with the objects on his cart.)*

FLOWER PAINTER. Elmer, Hazel—are you finished with your chores?

HAZEL. We have a problem.

IRIS. The spots are missing.

ELMER. I didn't take them.

FLOWER PAINTER. Did you talk to the Spot Maker?

HAZEL. He sent them out, just like he always does.

FLOWER PAINTER. But, the world requires Ladybugs, and Ladybugs must have their spots—

IRIS. Maybe you could paint them on. *(ELMER holds the Ladybugs out to the FLOWER PAINTER.)*

FLOWER PAINTER. Out of the question. I'm a Flower Painter—nothing more. I wouldn't know the first thing about painting spots on bugs.

ELMER *(happily)*. I guess our chores are done—

FLOWER PAINTER. It's not that simple, Elmer. Without us, the world would come to a standstill. If I abandoned my work, the flowers of the world would look like this— *(He produces a large, dull grey flower with a long stem.)* Instead of like this— *(A flourish of MUSIC as he makes several strokes with his paint brush and produces [seemingly] the same flower—now bright yellow and red.)* Now, you are Spotters and you must do your work.

HAZEL. But we've looked everywhere—

FLOWER PAINTER. I'm sure Iris can find them. She's like her dad in that way. That man could find the moon on the blackest of nights.

ELMER. Then why has he never found his way back home?

HAZEL *(a reprimand)*. Elmer—

ELMER. He's been gone forever.

FLOWER PAINTER. No one knows why, Elmer, and I think it's better left—

IRIS. Would you tell me if you knew? *(The FLOWER PAINTER stares at her.)* I was only a baby, then. Even my mom won't tell me why he left.

FLOWER PAINTER *(calmly, definitively)*. Because she *doesn't know*, Iris. No one does. It was the night of the Great Eclipse, and the moon was particularly hard to find. He went out to bring it in...and he's never returned.

IRIS. There's an eclipse tomorrow.

FLOWER PAINTER. The first one since that night. I doubt we'll get to enjoy it, though—

IRIS. Why not?

FLOWER PAINTER. The order just came and it's a big one.

HAZEL. An order for what?

FLOWER PAINTER. A *storm*.

ELMER. And it's a big one?

FLOWER PAINTER. Huge. *(He starts off, saying his farewell.)* Now and again.

ELMER, HAZEL, IRIS. Now and again.

HAZEL *(gently, to IRIS)*. Sorry about my brother. He says stupid things.

ELMER. I didn't mean—

IRIS. It's not stupid. I think about it all the time, too.

ELMER. I know what would make you feel better, Iris.

HAZEL. Helping us find those spots.

ELMER. Better than that. The order has come and a storm must be assembled. Now, what does this mean to people like you and me?

IRIS. It means that somewhere in this town...right now... just *waiting for us*...is a big...fresh...wet...batch of...

IRIS, HAZEL, ELMER *(a delicious whisper).* ...rain. *(They sigh with delight.)*

HAZEL. I bet the Rain Makers have been working non-stop—

ELMER. And it's just *sitting there*, and no one's—

HAZEL. Played in it, or—

ELMER. Tasted it, or—

IRIS. Race you there— *(As they begin to rush off they are stopped by the MEMORY MENDER, who pushes his cart in their path.)*

MEMORY MENDER. Careful, now—or you'll trip and rip your coats. And if you rip your coats I'll have to sew 'em back up for you. And you know why, don't you?

IRIS, ELMER, HAZEL *(having heard this a million times).* Yes, we know why—

MEMORY MENDER *(quickly, quizzing them).* Hazel, who are the rulers of Nocturno, our home?

HAZEL. The Great Goods.

MEMORY MENDER. Iris, where do the Great Goods live?

IRIS. Across the water, on Great Island.

MEMORY MENDER. And, Elmer, how deep is the water that surrounds Great Island?

ELMER. Umm—

IRIS. I know!

HAZEL. I know, too!

ELMER *(sharp, to the girls)*. So do I.

MEMORY MENDER. Well?

ELMER. It's—umm—

MEMORY MENDER. You knew it when I asked you last week.

ELMER. It's—oh, I don't know. Why do I always get the hard questions?!

MEMORY MENDER. Let me see your coat. *(ELMER walks over to the MENDER, who discovers a tiny rip in the sleeve of ELMER's PastCoat. He sews it back up as he speaks.)* See there. A little rip in your coat and your memory is harmed. It makes me crazy. You've got to take care of your coat because your coat holds your *past*. Every stitch, every pocket, every button and sleeve—it's your whole life in there! Think you can just go out and get a past like you can get a glass of milk?! Think again. *(He is finished sewing Elmer's coat).* There we are. Now, Elmer, how deep is the water that surrounds Great Island?

ELMER *(touching the new stitches in his coat)*. Ninety-nine thousand and twenty-three feet.

MEMORY MENDER. Exactly. Now, don't trip and get a rip. *(To IRIS, referring to her coat.)* Iris, have your mom keep an eye on that button. It's getting loose.

IRIS. I will.

MEMORY MENDER *(taking IRIS aside)*. And one thing more: The Fog Lifter is retiring today. After all these years, she can still set the fog down in the morning—but she just can't lift it up anymore. She'd like you to take her place, Iris.

IRIS *(honored)*. Thank you.

MEMORY MENDER. Now and again.

IRIS, ELMER, HAZEL. Now and again.

(MUSIC, as the MEMORY MENDER exits, pushing his cart, and LIGHTS SHIFT to reveal the LEAF MONITOR—Hazel and Elmer's mom—standing near a tree. She holds several large leaves and a clipboard. Near her are two large sacks with leaves protruding out of the tops of each. One is marked "OLD" and one is marked "NEW." IRIS, ELMER and HAZEL rush past her.)

LEAF MONITOR. Hazel. *(HAZEL stops. ELMER and IRIS also stop, and stand behind her.)* Where are you going?

HAZEL *(innocently)*. What, Mom?

LEAF MONITOR. You heard me. Where are you rushing off to? Did you finish your chores?

HAZEL. Why don't you ever ask Elmer that question?

LEAF MONITOR. Because you're the oldest.

ELMER. And you always will be. *(HAZEL glares at ELMER.)*

LEAF MONITOR. I need you to help me balance these books. I keep checking and double-checking, but I'm still *one leaf off.*

ELMER *(quickly)*. I didn't take it.

LEAF MONITOR. In all my years as the Leaf Monitor, I've never encountered this. We must be certain that for every new leaf we put on a tree, an old one falls. *(To HAZEL.)* But where could the missing one be?

(The THUNDER BOTTLERS enter, pushing a tall crate on wheels which is marked: "THUNDER." Stacked inside

the crate are bottles, sealed with bright red lids. Other bottles in the crate are empty and unsealed. The men are busy bottling the thunder, as follows: Holding a bottle to their mouths, they use a funnel of some kind and make a loud, vocal SOUND of thunder into the bottle. Then they quickly seal up the bottle with a red lid and place it inside the crate. They repeat this, throughout the following:)

THUNDER BOTTLER ONE. How many is that?

THUNDER BOTTLER TWO. That's thirty-four thunders.

THUNDER BOTTLER ONE. And that's not enough?!

THUNDER BOTTLER TWO. The order was for a forty-thunder storm.

ELMER. I've never seen so much thunder.

THUNDER BOTTLER TWO. We've been bottling it up all night.

THUNDER BOTTLER ONE. Gonna be a monster. *(He thunders into a bottle.)*

THUNDER BOTTLER TWO. We gotta be ready. *(He thunders into a bottle.)*

THUNDER BOTTLER ONE. Word is the Color Mixer has outdone himself. For this storm, he's come up with a brand new shade of *stormy sky blue-black.*

IRIS. Really?

THUNDER BOTTLE TWO. Gonna be something. *(He thunders into a bottle.)*

THUNDER BOTTLER ONE. We gotta be ready. *(He thunders into a bottle.)*

LEAF MONITOR *(to BOTTLER ONE).* Keep an eye out for a missing leaf.

THUNDER BOTTLER ONE. Did you take it, Elmer?

ELMER. Why does everyone always—

LEAF MONITOR. Once the storm comes and they start *swirling*—I'm afraid I'll never find it.

THUNDER BOTTLER TWO. It's not the BEST leaf that's missing, I hope.

HAZEL. Why not?

LEAF MONITOR. The BEST leaf must be sent to the Great Goods. You know that.

THUNDER BOTTLER ONE. Have Iris help you—if it's lost, she'll find it.

(The BOLT BENDER enters, carrying a piece of lightning about four feet long. He's bending it in various ways, trying to get the right shape. Other lighting bolts poke out of a quiver he wears over his shoulder.)

THUNDER BOTTLER ONE *(greeting the BOLT BENDER)*. Almost day.

BOLT BENDER *(nods, greets them ALL)*. Almost day, indeed—and I can't get the lightning right. Even the best Bolt Bender gets tired of making the same old lightning bolt, over and over again.

IRIS. But when there's thunder, people expect lightning to go with it.

BOLT BENDER. But why couldn't it be something else?

ELMER. Like what?

BOLT BENDER. Open up one of those thunders and let's experiment. Instead of a *lightning bolt* lighting up the sky, maybe it's— *(The BOLT BENDER reaches into his quiver, as BOTTLER ONE opens up one of the sealed bottles of thunder. A huge, quick crack of thunder fills the theatre, as the BOLT BENDER produces a bolt in the shape of a cactus—or some other incongruous ob-*

ject—and holds it high above his head. If possible, it lights up.) —THIS!

THUNDER BOTTLER ONE. That's a possibility.

THUNDER BOTTLER TWO *(holding up the original lightning bolt).* The Great Goods would never approve. As long as they've been our rulers, the lightning has always looked like *this. (With seriousness.)* And, believe me, you don't want to get on the bad side of the Great Goods.

HAZEL. What can happen to you?

THUNDER BOTTLER ONE *(directly to HAZEL).* If you disobey the Goods, your punishment is great.

HAZEL. Mom. *(HAZEL reaches into her PastCoat and brings out a large, beautiful autumn leaf.)* I'm sorry. I didn't mean to offend the Goods. But it was so pretty.

ELMER. It's the best leaf of them all. *(The LEAF MONITOR holds out her hand, and—reluctantly—HAZEL hands her the leaf. The LEAF MONITOR gently brushes a strand of hair from HAZEL's face.)*

LEAF MONITOR. Someday, Hazel, when *you're* the Leaf Monitor—you'll understand. Now, finish up your chores. It's almost day. *(The LEAF MONITOR exits, as the BOLT BENDER lifts the lightning bolt, saying—)*

BOLT BENDER *(as he leaves).* It's gonna be huge.

THUNDER BOTTLER ONE & TWO *(as they leave).* We gotta be ready. *(The BOTTLERS thunder into their bottles and leave, along with the BOLT BENDER.)*

ELMER *(whispers to IRIS and HAZEL).* Come on, it's our last chance before the storm.

(The KIDS rush away and arrive at a very large rain barrel. It is wooden, with notches on its side [or a ladder] which enables it to be climbed. A large label on the

*barrel reads: "*RAIN. *Batch #7893392." The KIDS see the barrel. They stop, stunned. ALL take a deep breath and are about to cheer loudly with delight—but realize they might be heard and get caught—so they exhale by quieting each other.)*

IRIS, HAZEL, ELMER *(to each other)*. SSSSSSSSShhhh-hhhhhhhh! *(They approach the barrel, looking around to make sure they're not being seen. They each roll their pant legs up a little ways. They begin to climb up the side/back of the barrel. Their voices remain soft, urgent.)*

HAZEL & ELMER *(to themselves, overlapping each other)*. Please don't let my mom call my name—please don't let my mom call my name—please don't let my mom call my name—please don't let—

IRIS. Hey, Hazel.

HAZEL. Yeah?

IRIS. Why is that?

HAZEL. Why is what?

IRIS. Why is it that no matter how far away from our mom we get, if she says our name—we can still hear her?

HAZEL. I don't know. But I wish we could *change it.*

ELMER. Let me ask you both a question: Are we going to *gab*...or are we going to *splash*?! *(IRIS and HAZEL nod. ALL climb up and then stop—looking down into the barrel below them. They look at each other. They each pull back one of their sleeves, exposing the whole of their arm. They take a deep breath—then they shove their arms down into the freezing cold water.)*

IRIS, HAZEL, ELMER *(a joyous scream)*. AAAAAAAA-AAAAUUUUUUUUUGGGGGGGGGGGHHHHHHHHHH! *(They laugh. They shiver. They cup their hands and drink water [which we see] from the barrels. They laugh and play some more, splashing a bit of water on each other, all the while repeating, under their breath, overlapping.)* Please don't let my mom call my name—please don't let my mom call my name—please don't let my—

(Shafts of LIGHT discover Iris' MOM, and the LEAF MONITOR, or their AMPLIFIED VOICES are heard.)

IRIS' MOM *(simultaneously)*. Iris!
LEAF MONITOR *(simultaneously)*. Hazel and Elmer!

IRIS' MOM & LEAF MONITOR. Time to come home!
    (The KIDS freeze, poised over the water, exasperated.)
IRIS, ELMER, HAZEL. HOW DO THEY *DO* THAT?!

(MUSIC, as the RAIN MAKER backs onto the stage, not seeing the KIDS. He wears a long apron covered with bright raindrops. He holds bright orange batons in his hands—and is using them to direct an unseen approaching cloud into place.)

RAIN MAKER *(backing in)*. Okay, let's back her on in. Good. Little to your left. Good. Man, they keep building these clouds bigger and bigger. I don't know how they even get off the ground. Okay. Good. Keep her coming— *(The KIDS have climbed down from the barrels, unseen.)*
IRIS *(whispering)*. Now and again.
HAZEL & ELMER. Now and again. *(They run off in separate directions and are gone.)*
RAIN MAKER. Okay, fellas. Let's load 'er up. We got some rain to drop.

(MUSIC CHANGES to what will become recognized as the "Still Life" music, as LIGHTS REVEAL Iris' home. It consists, in total, of a white wooden table with three white chairs. On the table is a simple vase. Nothing else. IRIS arrives home. Just before entering the scene, she stops and rolls her pant legs back down. As she does so, she watches, unseen, as her MOM puts an iris in the vase and sets a steaming cup of cocoa on the table. She pulls IRIS' chair away from the table. She goes to the middle chair and touches it, looks down at it. Then, she moves to her own chair, pulls it away from the table, and sits. She looks at the iris in the vase, admiring it. Note: This is the "Still Life"—the image that IRIS will remember throughout the play. IRIS stares at this picture for a long moment, as the music plays, then she enters.)

IRIS. Hi, Mom.

MOM. How was the rain?

IRIS. What rain? *(MOM looks at her.)* Good. Cold. *(MOM smiles. IRIS sits, the cocoa in front of her.)* Mom, they asked me to be the Fog Lifter.

MOM *(knowing this in advance).* I'm very proud of you, Iris.

IRIS. And we saw all the thunder they're bottling up.

MOM. This storm means a lot of extra work for me. A lot of wind to be taught.

IRIS. Why doesn't the wind remember how to whistle?

MOM. The wind has no memory. Just like us if we lost our PastCoats. So every storm, I've got to start from scratch. And, this being a big storm, I've got to teach not only whistling—but *howling.*

IRIS. Did Dad used to help you? *(Silence. MOM stares at her.)*

MOM. Yes, in fact, he did.

IRIS. And did you ever help him?

MOM. Iris, I've told you, it's better forgotten, it's better not to think about—

IRIS. Did he leave because of me? *(Pause, MOM stares at her.)* Because he didn't want to be my dad?

MOM *(gently)*. No.

IRIS. Why, then?

MOM. I wish I knew. On the night of the Great Eclipse he went in search of the moon—but it was so dark, Iris. I'm afraid he lost his way and was captured by that black night. I stood at the door, waiting for him—but all that arrived was the wind... moving through the house, not making a sound. Your dad was gone.

IRIS *(moving into the center chair)*. I know you haven't forgotten him. I know he's still part of your coat. *(IRIS touches MOM's coat near her heart.)* Please, Mom. Tell me about him. *(Silence. MOM looks at her, then speaks, a reverie.)*

MOM. Every night he roped the moon. And he pulled it down out of the sky. Then he'd give the signal— *(Palm open, fingers spread, arm extended—she raises her hand slowly in front of her.)* —to raise the sun into place. That was his job. He was the Day Breaker. *(Silence, as IRIS smiles at the memory—then grows more serious.)*

IRIS. There's another eclipse tomorrow.

MOM. Yes, there is.

IRIS. And who will find the moon? *(MOM stares at IRIS for a long moment.)*

MOM. He left something for you, Iris. A leather pouch. He
  wore it every night while he worked.

IRIS. Why haven't you ever given it to me?

MOM. I was afraid it would make you sad. All these years
  I've tried to protect you from that.

IRIS *(simply)*. Please don't. Not anymore. *(MOM stares at
  her, then gently touches IRIS' face.)*

MOM. You're right. It's time it was yours. *(MOM starts to
  exit, as IRIS lifts her cocoa from the table.)* Careful.
  That's hot. *(IRIS nods and sips the cocoa. Then she
  speaks to MOM offstage.)*

IRIS. Sometimes I get mad at him, Mom. Sometimes I
  wish I could find him and make him tell me why he left.
  I've waited so long for him to come home.

*(MUSIC UNDER, as from the direction MOM exited, the
MAN we saw earlier enters. His name is MISTER MAT-
TERNOT.)*

MISTER MATTERNOT. Your waiting is over, Iris. *(IRIS
  turns and sees MATTERNOT.)* You've been selected.

IRIS. Mom—?

MISTER MATTERNOT. You needn't call for your mother.
  You needn't think of your father, anymore—

IRIS *(growing more frightened)*. What are you doing here?
  You were lost—you were looking for someone— *(MAT-
  TERNOT approaches IRIS.)*

MISTER MATTERNOT. And I've found her.

IRIS. But I don't know who you are— *(IRIS tries to run off
  to find her MOM. MATTERNOT stands in her way.)*
  MOM!

MISTER MATTERNOT. You're a special girl, Iris. I'm told you can find missing things. *(IRIS is confused, scared, staring up at MATTERNOT.)*

IRIS. Yes, but I don't—

MISTER MATTERNOT. And because you are special, you've been chosen.

IRIS. Chosen by whom?

MISTER MATTERNOT. Why, by the rulers of Nocturno—the Great Goods. No one can travel to Great Island without their permission. But you, Iris, have been chosen to make the voyage.

IRIS. I don't want to visit Great Island. I want to know what's happened to my mom, where did she—?

MISTER MATTERNOT. Listen to me, Iris, you have not been chosen to *visit* Great Island. You have been chosen to *live there*.

IRIS. Live there? What are—?

MISTER MATTERNOT. They have, you see, only the BEST of everything on Great Island—but, until this moment, they have never had a little girl. Now, they will have you. You will be their daughter.

IRIS. I don't want to be their daughter! *(IRIS runs again in the direction her MOM left.)* I belong here with my mom—!

(As IRIS says this, MOM appears and faces her. She looks the same as before, however, she is not wearing her PastCoat. IRIS throws her arms around MOM, desperately. MOM does not respond at first, but then puts her arms gently around IRIS, sympathetically. IRIS is crying, holding tightly onto MOM as she speaks.)

IRIS. Make him go away! He's scaring me— I don't want to go to Great Island—please, Mom, make him go away! *(MUSIC FADES OUT, as MOM continues to hold IRIS.)*

MOM *(to MATTERNOT, concerned).* Why is this girl calling for her mother? Isn't there something we can do? Where is her family? Where is her home?

IRIS *(pulling away).* What are you saying? What is— *(For the first time, IRIS notices that her MOM's PastCoat is gone. She speaks, quietly.)* Mom. Where's your coat?

MOM. What's that?

IRIS *(to MATTERNOT).* Her coat—where is it?

MOM. What coat is she talking about?

IRIS. She went in there to bring me a pouch—a leather pouch—and now she—

MOM *(holds out the old and weathered leather pouch).* You must mean *this.* I found it in the next room. Is it yours? *(MATTERNOT takes the pouch from MOM.)*

IRIS *(desperately).* Yes. It belonged to my dad—

MISTER MATTERNOT. Iris, listen to me, the Great Goods do not wish to cause you any pain. And so, to remove the heartache, we must remove the coats. *(IRIS wraps her PastCoat tightly around herself. She backs away, crying.)*

IRIS. No. You can't. The Memory Mender said "Never let anything happen to your coat, or you'll be lost, you won't know who you are or—"

MOM *(overlapping, to MATTERNOT).* If the little girl wants to keep her coat, I think she should be allowed to—

MISTER MATTERNOT. Iris, I want to tell you something—

IRIS. Stay away from me—

MISTER MATTERNOT. Iris—

IRIS *(looking at MOM)*. YOU'VE TAKEN AWAY HER COAT—

MOM *(to MATTERNOT)*. We should find her mother. We should take her home.

IRIS *(crying)*. LOOK AT HER! SHE DOESN'T KNOW WHO I AM!

MISTER MATTERNOT *(grabbing her, holding her)*. IRIS. *(Quieter now.)* Listen to me. *This is what's done.* I don't like it, but it's what the Great Goods desire and therefore it must be done. Believe me, it's better to let me have your coat. If you keep it, you will be haunted by your past. You will think of your mother all the time. You will think of your home and your friends and your life here—and *you will never stop missing it.* It will be an ache that will never vanish from your heart. *(She looks up at him, holding her PastCoat tightly around her. MATTERNOT now reaches out his hands to her, asking for the coat.)* Now ... please.

IRIS. But if you take my past, who will I be?

MISTER MATTERNOT. You will be Iris. You'll be the girl you are now, but you'll remember nothing that happened before this moment.

IRIS. I'll never think of my mother again?

MISTER MATTERNOT. And, therefore, you'll never be saddened by your loss. *(Looking at MOM.)* Nor will she. *(To IRIS.)* It's the only way, Iris. It's the only way to make it not hurt.

IRIS *(stares at him)*. Let me keep the pouch.

MISTER MATTERNOT. Iris—

IRIS. Please?

MISTER MATTERNOT. It will mean nothing to you once your coat is gone.

IRIS. *Please? (MATTERNOT hands her the pouch. She attaches it around her waist, or over her shoulder. Then, she looks over at MOM, with some final hope of recognition.)* Mom ... ?

MOM *(kindly).* I do hope you find her, Iris. Whoever she is. Wherever she's gone. *(IRIS looks back at MATTERNOT. He holds out his hand, awaiting the coat. She stares at him. She looks down at her coat. She looks over at her MOM, one final time. She wraps her Past-Coat around herself very tightly for a moment ... closing her eyes ... And then, eyes still closed, she slowly removes her coat and holds it out away from her. A long, mournful gust of wind is heard, as MATTERNOT takes the coat in his arms. He then goes to the table and removes the iris from the vase. The table and chairs are taken away. The sound of wind fades. IRIS' eyes remain closed. The three of them stand there in silence for a moment. Then, finally, MATTERNOT speaks.)*

MISTER MATTERNOT *(gently).* Iris. Open your eyes. *(IRIS opens her eyes. He stands before her, speaks kindly.)* My name is Mister Matternot.

IRIS *(pleasantly).* Hello.

MISTER MATTERNOT. And this is Miss Overlook.

MISS OVERLOOK [formerly MOM]. Hello, Iris. It's a pleasure to meet you.

IRIS. It's nice to meet you, too. Where are we?

MISTER MATTERNOT. A little girl and her mother once lived here. We came to visit them. But now we're on our way to Great Island.

IRIS. Why's it called that?

MISTER MATTERNOT. Because everything on the island—every single thing—is the BEST of its kind. And
you, Iris, will continue that tradition.

IRIS *(looking at the pouch)*. And what's this?

MISS OVERLOOK. That's your pouch, Iris. It belongs to
you.

MISTER MATTERNOT. One thing more. *(He holds up
IRIS' PastCoat.)*

IRIS. What a wonderful coat. Is that mine, too?

MISTER MATTERNOT. It belonged to the little girl who
lived here. *(Testing her.)* Would you like it?

IRIS. Really?

MISTER MATTERNOT. She won't be needing it anymore.
Would you like to wear it?

IRIS. Is it cold where we're going?

MISTER MATTERNOT. Not at all. The temperature on
Great Island is always perfect.

IRIS *(simply)*. Then I won't need it. Thank you, anyway.

MISTER MATTERNOT *(smiles)*. As you wish. *(To OVER-
LOOK.)* Miss Overlook, I'll see you on Great Island.
*(MATTERNOT exits, taking the PastCoat with him. IRIS
begins to follow him as OVERLOOK sees something on
the ground. She reaches down and picks it up: it is a
button from Iris' PastCoat.)*

MISS OVERLOOK. Iris? *(IRIS stops, turns back to her.)*
Did you drop this? *(She holds up the button.)*

IRIS. What is it?

MISS OVERLOOK. It's a button.

IRIS. It must have fallen off that girl's coat.

MISS OVERLOOK *(hands IRIS the button)*. Why don't
you hold on to it. Maybe you'll find her in your travels.

IRIS. I'll put it in my pouch.

MISS OVERLOOK. I hope I see you again, Iris.

*(IRIS nods and watches MISS OVERLOOK exit. IRIS
starts to put the button in her pouch. She stops, looks at
the button, holding it in front of her. She closes her eyes.
She rubs the button between her thumb and forefinger.
As she does so MUSIC PLAYS—the same music we
heard under the "Still Life" earlier—and—LIGHTS
SHIFT, isolating only IRIS and a [perhaps] miniature
"Still Life," the table, cocoa, and the iris in its vase,
suspended in mid-air above the stage. The rest of the
stage is in darkness. IRIS does not look at the "Still
Life"—instead, she closes her eyes, tightly, once again.
As she continues to rub the button, the light on the "Still
Life" grows brighter and brighter. Then, as she opens
her eyes and puts the button back in her pouch, the
"Still Life" goes suddenly black. It is gone. MUSIC
OUT, as MISTER MATTERNOT reappears, quickly, say-
ing—)*

MISTER MATTERNOT. We're due at one o'clock, Iris,
and we mustn't be late. Are you ready?
IRIS. Ready!

*(IRIS runs off. MISTER MATTERNOT follows her, as
MUSIC PLAYS, and LIGHTS REVEAL the Great Room
of the Great Goods. HIS MOST EXCELLENT, GROTTO
GOOD stands in the room. His dashingly elegant clothes
have one button, one pocket, one tassel of fringe. He
wears one shoe, only. He holds a monocle in his hand,
which he uses from time to time. He speaks to his ser-
vant, MISTER OTHERGUY—dressed in the same som-*

*ber manner as MATTERNOT and wearing a similar sort
of tool belt—who is hurriedly dusting everything in the
room with a single-feather duster. MUSIC UNDER and
OUT.)*

GROTTO GOOD. But, my fear is this, that I will handle it
    badly. I fear I don't know how to *maintain* a little girl.
    What do they *do*? What do they eat? And what will I do
    if she *says something to me*?
MISTER OTHERGUY. I'm sure you'll handle it well,
    Master Good.
GROTTO GOOD. Shouldn't they be here? It's nearly one
    o'clock.

*(HER MOST EXCELLENT, GRETTA GOOD enters. She
is dressed in a similarly elegant style to her husband.
She, too, wears only one shoe. She has one ring on her
finger. She is affixing her one earring as she arrives.)*

GRETTA GOOD. I must tell you, a terrifying thing just
    happened to me.
GROTTO GOOD. What was it, my dear?
GRETTA GOOD. I found a *second earring*. It was just ly-
    ing there, next to this one.
GROTTO GOOD. My good, what did you do?
GRETTA GOOD. I threw it away, instantly.
GROTTO GOOD. Oh, thank good.
GRETTA GOOD. It set me back, I must tell you. A shock
    like that.
GROTTO GOOD. Don't think of it again. Now, Gretta
    dear, I've been assured by Mister Otherguy that I
    needn't be nervous about meeting a little girl.

GRETTA GOOD. We'll be fine, Grotto dear. We've chosen the best of the best.

GROTTO GOOD. But what do they *do*—these *children*? That's all I'd like to know. And what if she says *something to me*? (*GRETTA shrugs: "I don't know."*) Mister Otherguy? (*OTHERGUY shrugs—imitating GRETTA.*) Oh, my good.

(*The door flies open quickly, revealing IRIS. She now wears an overlayer of clothing which is similar to the Great Goods—elegantly eccentric, very different from her Nocturno attire. She wears one very shiny shoe. The GOODS gesture for her to take a step into the room. She does so. She stands stiffly, with a pleasant, forced smile on her face. The clock chimes, once. For a moment, they all just stand and nod at each other. Finally, IRIS turns to GROTTO and speaks in as friendly a way as possible.*)

IRIS. Hello. I'm Iris. What an odd place this is. (*GROTTO nods at her for a moment, then turns quickly to OTHERGUY.*)

GROTTO GOOD. My good, *she said something to me.* (*OTHERGUY gestures for GROTTO to respond. GROTTO looks at IRIS, looks at GRETTA, looks back to IRIS...then finally speaks, smilingly, definitively.*) You are a girl.

IRIS. Yes.

GROTTO GOOD (*smiling throughout*). And now you are here.

IRIS. Yes, I am.

GROTTO GOOD. And I am speaking to you.

IRIS. Yes, you are.

GROTTO GOOD *(still smiling)*. And now I am finished. *(Turns to his wife.)* Gretta?

GRETTA GOOD *(walks toward IRIS, calmly)*. You must forgive my husband. He's never spoken to a little girl before. You are the first one to ever arrive on Great Island.

IRIS. I see.

GRETTA GOOD. But you are welcome here, Iris. More than welcome, you are *treasured*.

GROTTO GOOD. You will now be the greatest of our goods.

GRETTA GOOD. Have you nothing to say?

IRIS. Umm...thank you...

GRETTA GOOD. And?

IRIS. And where's my other shoe?

GROTTO GOOD. Oh, my.

GRETTA GOOD. You are wearing the finest shoe under the sky. Have you *looked* at it?

IRIS. Yes, I have, and it's beautiful—maybe the most beautiful shoe I've ever seen but, still, one of them is missing and the one I'm wearing really hurts my foot. Is there another pair I could wear?

GROTTO GOOD. Oh, my.

IRIS. They don't have to be as nice as these—

GROTTO GOOD. Oh, my.

IRIS. Just a little more comfortable, so I can—

GRETTA GOOD. Iris.

IRIS. Yes, Mother Good?

GRETTA GOOD. There are no other shoes for you. We have only what's BEST on this island and to ensure the value and importance of each item, *we have only one of everything. (To OTHERGUY.)* Bring her something to drink. *(OTHERGUY nods and brings a goblet, as well as a small, sealed glass container, on a tray to IRIS.)*

IRIS. One of everything—what do you mean?

GROTTO GOOD. Look around, Iris! Everything here is unrivaled in its goodness. Like, for example, our BOOK. Or this—our DRAPE. Or our CHAIR.

IRIS. You only have one chair?

GROTTO GOOD. Isn't it a beauty? *(He brings it to her and insists she sit in it during the following:)*

GRETTA GOOD. So, you see, Iris, that is why you have only one shoe.

IRIS. What happened to its mate?

GROTTO GOOD. It is now in the Tunnel of the Un-Wanted.

GRETTA GOOD *(sees that IRIS' drink is ready)*. Oh, here we are. Thirsty?

IRIS. Very. *(OTHERGUY offers IRIS the goblet. She takes it and looks in it—it is empty. OTHERGUY opens the sealed glass container. He tips it over and pours its contents into the goblet: one long, slow, perfect drop of water. The GOODS nod approvingly, as IRIS looks into the goblet.)* What is this?

GROTTO GOOD. It's a perfect raindrop.

IRIS. This is all the water you have?

GRETTA GOOD. It's all we need. For, at daybreak, another perfect drop will arrive. There's a land near here, where they work all night to see to our pleasure each day.

GROTTO GOOD. So, drink up! *(IRIS looks at them, looks at the goblet, then drinks. She, of course, barely tastes it. As she swallows, the GOODS sigh, audibly, blissfully.)*

GRETTA GOOD. Perfect, isn't it?

IRIS. I guess.

GRETTA GOOD. Now, Iris, we've heard you have a gift for finding things. Is that true?

IRIS. I don't know. Maybe. I don't remember finding *anything*.

GROTTO GOOD. You'll help us find PERFECT THINGS for the island, I'm sure. Now, we've prepared the best of the best for you—

IRIS. What exactly do you *do* here?

GRETTA GOOD. We enjoy our goods in the greatest of ways.

IRIS. Don't you work?

GROTTO GOOD. Certainly not.

GRETTA GOOD. But we are ever on the lookout for flaws. We mustn't let anything that is not the BEST invade Great Island. *(GRETTA sees the pouch which IRIS wears.)* Like *this* for example. What is the meaning of this old pouch?

GROTTO GOOD. And what's inside?

IRIS. A button. It belongs to a little girl I'm looking for.

GROTTO GOOD. There are no other girls, Iris. You're the only one here.

GRETTA GOOD. Mister Otherguy, show Iris her toy box. *(OTHERGUY raises the lid of the toy box, as IRIS continues to stare at GROTTO.)*

IRIS. There's no one else to play with?

GRETTA GOOD. We're still searching for a little boy.

GROTTO GOOD. One who's perfect—like you.

IRIS. You brought me here because you think I'm perfect?

GROTTO GOOD. Of course we did.

IRIS. I'm not perfect.

GRETTA GOOD *(after a quick look at GROTTO)*. *Really?*

IRIS. Not perfect at all.

GROTTO GOOD. Very well. Tell us something you've done that *wasn't perfect*. Some day when you did a bad thing. Something from your *past*, Iris. *(The GOODS look at her.)* Well? *(Silence. IRIS thinks.)*

IRIS. I can't think of anything.

GROTTO GOOD. You see!

IRIS. But, I know I'm not— *(The GOODS leave happily, in a flourish, saying—)*

GROTTO GOOD. Enjoy your toys, Iris!

GRETTA GOOD. And if you find anything that is not the BEST of its kind—

GROTTO GOOD. We'll discard and replace it immediately!

GRETTA GOOD. A great good pleasure to meet you!

GROTTO GOOD. A great good pleasure, indeed!

(MUSIC, as LIGHTS PULL DOWN to isolate IRIS near the toy box. The face of the clock remains lit, as well. MISTER OTHERGUY lifts something out of the toy box: a doll encased in glass. On the side of the glass is a small lock. The doll is dressed identically to IRIS. OTHERGUY holds the doll out to IRIS. IRIS looks at him...then takes it from him. She looks at the doll, then tries to open the lock to take the doll from the case—but it won't open.)

IRIS. It's locked. How can I play with her if she's locked inside?

(MISTER OTHERGUY simply shrugs and exits. MUSIC builds as IRIS sits on the closed toy box, her hands

pressed against the glass that houses the doll, as the
face of the clock grows brighter and brighter. The clock
chimes, once. LIGHTS RISE fully on the room, once
again, as MISTER MATTERNOT enters.)

MISTER MATTERNOT. Hello, Iris.

IRIS. What day is it today?

MISTER MATTERNOT. It's the BEST day of the week—
just like it always is.

IRIS. And how long have I been here?

MISTER MATTERNOT. You've been on Great Island for
one month—the BEST month of the year. *(IRIS is silent.*
She takes off her lone shoe and tosses it aside.) Is something wrong? Are you unhappy?

IRIS. I don't remember being happier and I don't remember being sadder. But there must have been a time when
I had someone to play with.

MISTER MATTERNOT. Iris, the Goods have filled your
toy box with the finest toys under the— *(IRIS finishes*
his sentence with him, as she goes to the toy box and
pulls out the following items as she describes them.)

IRIS *(simultaneous with MATTERNOT).* "—finest toys under the sky." Yes, I know—and maybe *you'd* like to
play with them. Would you like to play cards, well...
here's the CARD. Or maybe you'd like to do a jigsaw
puzzle, well...here's the PIECE.

MISTER MATTERNOT. What is it you want to do, Iris?
(She now begins to play "Jacks"—with the ball and the
one—very beautiful—jack.)

IRIS. I want to—I don't know—I want to go fishing.

MISTER MATTERNOT. But the Goods have already
caught a fish—a remarkable fish—

IRIS. I don't care! I wouldn't mind TWO of something. Like maybe two jacks instead of one. Or maybe two kids that I could play with.

MISTER MATTERNOT. Perhaps you'd like to go *find* something—the perfect leaf, the perfect stone?

IRIS. There's no need— *(She holds up a picture frame. Framed within it is the leaf we saw HAZEL give to the LEAF MONITOR.)* The perfect leaf arrived today. Where do these things come from?

MISTER MATTERNOT. A land near here.

IRIS. Is that where the little girl lived? The girl whose coat you offered me?

MISTER MATTERNOT. I don't recall.

IRIS. Of course you do. She lived there with her mother. May we go see her?

MISTER MATTERNOT. She's gone, Iris.

IRIS. Where did she go?

MISTER MATTERNOT. She can't be found.

IRIS. But I need to return something to her.

MISTER MATTERNOT. Put it out of your mind.

IRIS. Show me the way— I'll find her myself.

MISTER MATTERNOT. I've told you: No one leaves the island without the permission of the Goods.

IRIS. Then I'll—

MISTER MATTERNOT. And the Goods intend to keep you here.

IRIS. Here in this room? Forever?

(MISTER MATTERNOT stares at her, saying nothing, as MISTER OTHERGUY and MISTER HIMTOO enter.)

MISTER OTHERGUY. Iris, the Goods have denied your request. *(IRIS lifts the doll still in the glass case and holds it.)*

MISTER MATTERNOT. What request?

IRIS. I asked for the key to unlock this case.

MISTER HIMTOO. She is to remain under glass.

MISTER OTHERGUY. It is the word of the Goods.

MISTER MATTERNOT *(attempting to cheer her)*. I'm sure you'll find a way to play with her, Iris. She's the BEST doll under the—

IRIS *(simply)*. My toy box does not suit me.

MISTER MATTERNOT *(thrown by this new tone in her voice)*. I beg your pardon?

IRIS. I am a Good now and I deserve the best of the best, isn't that correct?

MISTER MATTERNOT. Well, yes, of course, but—

IRIS. This box is flawed and I can no longer abide it. I want it replaced.

MISTER MATTERNOT. If I may ask...what is wrong with it?

IRIS. It...has TWO handles! One on either side! It's intolerable! The Goods asked me to tell them if something was not satisfactory—and this, clearly, is not. I want it replaced immediately. *(MATTERNOT stares at her, then turns to OTHERGUY and HIMTOO.)*

MISTER MATTERNOT. Inform the Goods. *(OTHERGUY and HIMTOO exit.)*

IRIS. Mister Matternot?

MISTER MATTERNOT. Yes?

IRIS. Why are there three of you?

MISTER MATTERNOT. What do you mean?

IRIS. You all work for the Goods. And they have only one
of everything. How come they have three of you?

MISTER MATTERNOT *(a fact, without pity)*. Because
we're ordinary. We're not special in the least. *(Pause,
going to her.)* It's only been one month, Iris. In time,
you'll come to love it here. *(She look up at him.)* What
better place could there be?

IRIS. I don't know. But there must be something. Somewhere. *(She removes the button from her pouch. As she
rubs it, MUSIC PLAYS and LIGHTS rise on the miniature "Still Life" once again.)* Because when I hold this
button in my hand and close my eyes...I see a picture in
my mind. Why would that happen?

MISTER MATTERNOT. May I see that button? *(IRIS
holds the button out to him. He removes his gloves and
takes hold of the button, inspecting it. The "Still Life" is
now gone. The MUSIC FADES OUT.)*

IRIS. And why don't I know what that picture means?

MISTER MATTERNOT *(gently, close to her)*. Iris. Some
things are the way they are because the way they are is
the least likely to bring sadness or bad memories.

IRIS. I don't have any bad memories. Do *you*? *(She sees
the open palms of his hands—still holding the button.
She touches one of his hands.)* You have scars on your
hand. Long, red scars. Where did they come from?
*(MATTERNOT looks at her, then quickly hands the but-
ton back to her—and pulls his gloves back over his
hands. He exits, as the GOODS' VOICES are heard, opposite.)*

VOICE OF GROTTO GOOD. OH, IRIS!

VOICE OF GRETTA GOOD. WE HAVE YOUR NEW TOY
BOX!

(IRIS looks off in the direction of their VOICES, then looks at the toy box next to her. An idea! She opens the toy box and climbs into it, closing the lid and disappearing just as the GOODS enter, followed by MISTER OTHERGUY and MISTER HIMTOO who carry a new, larger, more ornate toy box—with only one handle.)

GROTTO GOOD. Here we are!

GRETTA GOOD *(looking around)*. Iris?

GROTTO GOOD. She must be with Matternot. We'll leave it here and surprise her. *(As GRETTA speaks, GROTTO gestures to OTHERGUY and HIMTOO—showing them where the new toy box should be placed. They follow his instructions.)*

GRETTA GOOD. I'm so proud of her, Grotto. She found fault with something! She's become a Good through and through.

GROTTO GOOD *(points to the "old" toy box)*. Look at that—it's an abomination! Away with it this instant!

(MISTER OTHERGUY and MISTER HIMTOO lift, or roll, the "old" toy box—exchanging a quick, curious look regarding its weight—and then exit, taking it away, as MISTER MATTERNOT enters, passing them.)

GRETTA GOOD. Ah, there you are.

MISTER MATTERNOT. Where are they going? *(GROTTO is putting IRIS' toys—the puzzle piece, the card, etc., into the new toy box.)*

GROTTO GOOD. In with the best, out with the rest.

GRETTA GOOD. Is Iris with you?

MISTER MATTERNOT. No. I left her right here.

GRETTA GOOD. That's impossible. *(GROTTO spots IRIS' shoe on the ground.)*

GROTTO GOOD. Gretta.

GRETTA GOOD. What? *(GROTTO lifts the shoe.)* Oh, my good.

GROTTO GOOD. I fear she's escaped.

GRETTA GOOD. Escaped? But where would she go?

GROTTO GOOD. Every inch of the island must be searched.

GRETTA GOOD *(to MATTERNOT)*. Well, don't just stand there—

GRETTA & GROTTO GOOD. START SEARCHING!

(MUSIC, as LIGHTS SHIFT to night. A beach on Great Island. One very large seashell, or stone, is prominent, upstage. MUSIC FADES into the SOUND of waves. IRIS enters, exhausted, worried. She is barefoot. She looks around in all directions, calling out.)

IRIS. Hello! *(No answer.)* Is anybody out there, across the water?! *(No answer.)* Can you tell me where I am?! *(IRIS climbs atop the shell and calls out.)* HELLLOOOOO! *(An ECHO comes back to her from the water.)*

ECHO. HELLLOOOOO! *(IRIS looks into the distance, trying to locate the ECHO. Note: If possible, both live and re-corded voice are used to make the "echo" come from a variety of directions in the theatre.)*

IRIS. WHERE AM IIIIIII?

ECHO. WHERE AM IIIIIII? *(IRIS gradually climbs down and approaches the water, downstage. Liking the sound of the "IIIIIII"—she continues.)*

IRIS. IIIIIII!

ECHO. IIIIII!

IRIS. I!

ECHO. I!

IRIS. IIIIII'M—

ECHO. IIIIII'M—

IRIS. IIIIIIRIS!

ECHO. IIIIIIRIS!

IRIS. IIIIII'M IIIIIIRIS!

ECHO/VOICE OF ANNABEL LEE. IIIIII'M ANNABEL LEE!

IRIS *(jumps back away from the water's edge)*. Who's there?

VOICE OF ANNABEL LEE. An echo waiting to be free. *(IRIS stares into the distance, still unable to locate the VOICE.)*

IRIS. Can you help me get away from here? I'm lost.

VOICE OF ANNABEL LEE. Yes, we both seem to be.

IRIS. Really? Where do you live?

(ANNABEL LEE, a young woman of the sea, appears. She wears a tattered gown of dark blues and greens and the boots and belt of a pirate. Her belt holds a small telescope. Her hair is entwined with seaweed. And, most prominently, she has a long chain [or rope] attached to her wrist, or ankle with a large padlock, which leads far out into the sea, offstage. IRIS stares at her, amazed.)

ANNABEL LEE *(as she enters)*. In a kingdom by the sea. Have you never seen an Annabel Lee?

IRIS. Never. How did you—

ANNABEL LEE. For years I've been locked away—held against my will—but now you, Iris, will set me free.

IRIS. How?

ANNABEL LEE. By loosing these chains that bind me to the sea.

IRIS. But how did you get here?

ANNABEL LEE. Through your wishing, I assume. What else could it be?

IRIS. I did wish for someone to play with. And I wished for someone to help me get across this water.

ANNABEL LEE. And I wished I would find my ship.

IRIS. You have a ship?

ANNABEL LEE *(looking through her telescope)*. It's what I'm searching for, and my ship is searching for me.

IRIS. How do you know?

ANNABEL LEE. I listen at night, locked away, in my kingdom by the sea.
  And as the waves crash and fall—
  I can hear in the squall—
  My ship's voice calling to me—

IRIS. What does it say?

ANNABEL LEE. "For the moon never beams without bringing me dreams
  Of the beautiful Annabel Lee;
  And the stars never rise, but I see the bright eyes
  Of my captain, Annabel Lee."

IRIS *(smiles)*. Your ship really calls out to you?

ANNABEL LEE. I'm so close to finding it, Iris. It's just out of reach.

IRIS. I see a picture like that, sometimes. A picture of a room. But I don't know where it is.

ANNABEL LEE. What have you been using to navigate with? Have you been using the stars?

IRIS. There's more than *one*?

ANNABEL LEE. Of course there are. Look. *(She hands IRIS the telescope, and IRIS looks through it at a sky full of stars.)*

IRIS. Oh, my. From the palace of the Great Goods, you can only see *one* star.

ANNABEL LEE. Why is that?

IRIS. It's the best one. They chose it.

ANNABEL LEE. There's no best in stars. They're like waves upon the sea. A multitude of many; far as the eye can see. *(Shakes the chain with her arm.)* Now, if you'll free me from this, I'll find my ship and together we'll sail away. *(IRIS goes to her and tries to pry the lock from ANNABEL LEE's arm.)*

IRIS. It's locked shut. Maybe we could cut the chain.

ANNABEL LEE. It's too strong— I've tried.

IRIS *(looks closely at the lock)*. Then we have to pick the lock. We need something long and narrow and flat. *(IRIS looks around, but sees nothing that will work.)*

ANNABEL LEE. Maybe something in your pouch?

IRIS. No. *(Showing her.)* All I have is this button. *(Still looking.)* There must be *something* we can use—

ANNABEL LEE *(looking up to the sky)*. I think I know what it is.

IRIS. You do? *(ANNABEL LEE nods.)* What is it? *(ANNABEL LEE sits, leaning against the shell, looking up at the stars.)*

ANNABEL LEE. The same thing that brought me here to you.

IRIS. But that was just me—wishing.

ANNABEL LEE. Exactly. *(Gestures for IRIS to join her.)* C'mon, Iris. Your wishes will be our vessel. And the stars will be our map. And with courage and faith as our

captain and mate, the ship I've lost and room you seek
may fall into our lap.

(ANNABEL LEE begins to whistle "Twinkle Twinkle Lit-
tle Star," softly and beautifully. After a moment, IRIS
sits next to her and joins her. They whistle/hum the song
together, happily. As they are about to repeat the song,
they hear a PIANO playing the same melody, nearby.
They stop whistling/humming. They look around—not
knowing where it's coming from. As they stand up and
look around, the PIANO stops. IRIS and ANNABEL LEE
whistle/hum a phrase of the song, and the PIANO echoes
the phrase. Note: If possible, the PIANO phrases should
come from a variety of directions in the theatre, similar
to the "echo" earlier in this scene. IRIS and ANNABEL
LEE look around. Then they rush downstage and whis-
tle/hum a phrase of the song, and the PIANO echoes the
phrase. Still looking for the source, IRIS and ANNABEL
LEE rush upstage and whistle/hum the next phrase of the
song, and the PIANO again echoes the phrase, and then,
unseen—at first—by IRIS and ANNABEL LEE,
MOZART, age eleven, appears downstage, at the edge of
the water. He is playing a small piano which is attached
to his waist like a drum. The song is the "Twelve Piano
Variations in C" [which we know as "Twinkle Twinkle
Little Star"]. He is dressed in the clothes of his day. A
white handkerchief cascades from his breast pocket. In
between phrases, he repeatedly jumps back away from
the unseen waves and shakes water from his shoes—all
the while continuing to play, avidly. IRIS and ANNABEL
LEE turn and stare at him, curiously. They've never seen
a person like this before. MOZART finishes the song

*with a flourish, as ANNABEL LEE and IRIS—behind
him—applaud. MOZART turns, surprised.)*

MOZART. *Guten tag! Bon jour!* Good day! *(A quick look
up at the stars, speaks urgently.)* Or *night.* Why is it
night? How long has it been night? And how close are
we to morning? It's crucial that I find out. Can you tell me?!
IRIS. Who *are* you?
MOZART. Oh. Yes. Where are my manners? I must have
left them in Vienna where manners seem to be all that
matters. *(Steps toward them, bows.)* I am Mozart. Wolf-
gang Amadeus Mozart. *(IRIS and ANNABEL LEE mimic
his bow, as they speak, simultaneously.)*

IRIS. Hi.
ANNABEL LEE. Hello.

MOZART. But you can call me Motes. I prefer that. Where
are we?
IRIS. On the shores of Great Island.
ANNABEL LEE. Isn't it a beautiful beach?
MOZART *(sincerely, wiping away some water).* Yes—but
why must it be so close to the water?
IRIS *(smiles).* I'm Iris. And this is Annabel Lee.
MOZART. Are you a pirate?
ANNABEL LEE. My mother was.
MOZART. Your *mother* was?
ANNABEL LEE. And my father was the sea.
MOZART. And I thought *my* family was strange.
ANNABEL LEE. Why must you know when the night ends?
MOZART. I've been searching for something. Something
that's *just out of reach. (IRIS and ANNABEL LEE look*

at each other.) It's a song I work on at night. Only at night. *(With one finger, he plays the first few phrases of the Serenade in G—the Allegro movement from "Eine kleine Nachtmusik." He stops—abruptly—one note prior to completing the second phrase. He looks back at them.)* But, that's it. I can't seem to finish it, because when the sun rises... the melody vanishes. If only I could stop time—if only I could find a way to make the sun wait *just a few seconds more before rising*—I think the song would come to me.

ANNABEL LEE. I know that feeling. Something just out of reach, like my ship— *(IRIS removes the button from her pouch and shows it to them.)*

IRIS. Like when I hold this button in my hand. *(She closes her eyes, as the "Still Life" is illuminated once again. The MUSIC which accompanied it plays softly, under, as IRIS describes it.)* There is a table. And on the table, a vase. And in the vase, an iris.

MOZART. Is it a memory?

IRIS. I'm not sure. This button belonged to a little girl. If I can find her, maybe she'll tell me. *(The "Still Life" vanishes. The MUSIC FADES.)*

ANNABEL LEE. Is she on this island?

IRIS. I've looked everywhere—and I've found a lot of things for the Great Goods and I found the two of you— but I can't find that little girl.

MOZART *(as he searches once again for the final note of his melody)*. If she's that elusive, she must be worth the search. Like a melody which hovers in the ether— anonymous and unknown—until it is captured and rendered unforgettable.

IRIS *(looking at MOZART's tiny piano)*. That's it.

ANNABEL LEE. What? *(IRIS approaches MOZART and points to something on his piano.)*

IRIS. May I see that note?

MOZART. That is not, technically, a *note*. It is rather a *key*.

IRIS. Then, it's perfect. May I have it?

MOZART. *Have it?*

IRIS. Just for a moment—yes.

ANNABEL LEE. Iris, what are you—

MOZART. But I may need it. It may be part of the melody I'm searching for—

IRIS *(pointing to another one)*. Then give me that one—or that one—or that one. Surely you can do without one of your notes. *(MOZART looks at her, then chooses a key from the piano and hands her the thin, ivory top of it, saying—)*

MOZART *(reluctantly)*. Here. *(A reprimand.)* And, as I said, it is not, technically, called a *note*. It is—rather— *(IRIS inserts the piano key into ANNABEL LEE's lock, and frees her from the chain, saying—)*

IRIS. —a key.

ANNABEL LEE *(happily tossing the chain aside)*. Thank you, Iris! And thank you, Motes! Now, if we find my ship, we can go in search of that little girl.

MOZART. Did you say "ship"?

ANNABEL LEE. Yes.

MOZART. As in wood which floats precariously over deep, freezing water?

ANNABEL LEE. Yes.

MOZART *(moving away)*. Could you point me to Vienna?

ANNABEL LEE. Are you afraid of the water?

MOZART *(taking his "key" back from IRIS)*. I prefer to be anchored to a piano bench.

ANNABEL LEE. But water is like a rush of music—it is the common language of the world. *(To IRIS.)* Isn't that right, Iris?

IRIS. Well, I don't remember if—

ANNABEL LEE. When you're on the water, your heart pounds with delight. And your past is a tide which crashes inside and you speak aloud the story of your life. *(To IRIS.)* Isn't that so, Iris? *(Silence. IRIS stares at ANNABEL LEE.)*

IRIS. I can't say.

ANNABEL LEE. But, Iris—

IRIS. I have no story to tell.

MOZART. But what about your past? What's the first thing you remember?

IRIS. The face of Mister Matternot. A woman standing with him. And this button.

ANNABEL LEE. And that's all?

IRIS. That's all. *(A huge crash of thunder/crack of lightning, followed by the SOUND of rain. IRIS, ANNABEL LEE and MOZART stare at the sky in wonder.)*

MOZART. Look at that.

ANNABEL LEE. I've never seen the sky that color. What would you call that?

IRIS. Stormy sky blue-black.

ANNABEL LEE. It's so lovely.

MOZART. And so...wet. *(IRIS and ANNABEL LEE are about to playfully grab MOZART and push him toward the water, as a VOICE is heard, nearby.)*

VOICE OF MISTER MATTERNOT. IRIS? IRIS, IS THAT YOU? *(They freeze. ANNABEL LEE and MOZART turn to IRIS.)*

MOZART *(whispers)*. Who's that?

IRIS *(whispers)*. They'll take me back to the Great Goods.
ANNABEL LEE. Hide, Iris. We'll take care of it.
MOZART. We will?

(ANNABEL LEE gestures for MOZART—still wearing his piano—to run offstage. She then exits, opposite. IRIS hides behind the large shell, as MISTER MATTERNOT and MISTER OTHERGUY rush on, looking around.)

MISTER OTHERGUY. I heard her voice. I know I did.
MISTER MATTERNOT *(calling out)*. THE GOODS ARE VERY DISPLEASED WITH YOU, IRIS. *(No response.)* If you don't let me bring you home, I'm afraid they'll punish you. They'll throw you into the Tunnel of the Un-Wanted and you'll never be found again. *(No response.)* IRIS? *(OTHERGUY realizes IRIS must be behind the shell. He signals to MATTERNOT and they begin to approach the shell, slowly, from either side. As they are about to look behind it and find IRIS, a VOICE comes from a distant place, offstage.)*
VOICE OF ANNABEL LEE. Here I am! *(MATTERNOT and OTHERGUY turn in the direction of the VOICE. IRIS too, peeks up—briefly—from behind the shell.)*
MISTER OTHERGUY. Over there! *(MATTERNOT and OTHERGUY start to rush off in the direction of the VOICE, as a PIANO plays a quick phrase of MUSIC from a distant place, offstage, opposite. MATTERNOT and OTHERGUY stop, turn in the direction of the piano.)*
MISTER MATTERNOT. What was that? *(As MATTERNOT and OTHERGUY start to rush off in the direction of the PIANO, the VOICE OF ANNABEL LEE calling "Here I am!" and the phrase of Mozart MUSIC begin to repeat*

and overlap each other—coming from seemingly every possible direction all at once. MATTERNOT and OTHER-GUY freeze—trying to decide which way to go. They look at each other. They decide to split up and head off in opposite directions. They rush off, calling out.)

MISTER MATTERNOT & MISTER OTHERGUY. IRIS!

(As they disappear...the VOICE and PIANO fade away and are gone. Silence, as IRIS slowly emerges from behind the shell. She walks downstage, calling off to either side of the stage in a whispered voice.)

IRIS. It's safe. They're gone. *(Silence. IRIS looks around for them.)* You can come out now. *(Silence. She continues to look.)* Motes? Annabel Lee? *(Silence. She stares in disbelief, heartbroken.)* Oh, no. I made you up. *(IRIS sits on the ground, sadly.)* I made you up, and now you're gone—

(MUSIC UP, as suddenly ANNABEL LEE and MOZART are revealed, standing in the back of the theatre [or pop up from behind the shell]. They call out to IRIS, gesturing for her to follow them.)

ANNABEL LEE. Come on, Iris!

MOZART. Off we go! *(IRIS stands and breaks into a big smile as MUSIC CRESCENDOS, and LIGHTS SNAP OUT, quickly.)*

END OF ACT ONE

ACT TWO

SCENE: *MUSIC, as LIGHTS REVEAL a small, downstage area. MISTER MATTERNOT leads IRIS, MOZART and ANNABEL LEE onstage. They stand in a line, facing the audience, as MATTERNOT addresses them.*

MISTER MATTERNOT. The Goods will be with you in a moment. Please—for your own safety—wait here until they're ready for you. Great Island can be a dangerous place to get lost.

IRIS. We weren't lost, we were curious. And how can that be dangerous? If everything here is the BEST under the sky, what harm can befall us?

MISTER MATTERNOT. The Goods only allow the best of things to be *seen*. But, elsewhere on the island, hidden away in the Tunnel of the UnWanted, are all the OTHERS—all the angry, forgotten, discarded things which are common and unremarkable. You must take care to avoid them.

ANNABEL LEE. You don't understand. All she wants to do is—

MISTER MATTERNOT. Are you her friend?

ANNABEL LEE. Yes, I am.

MISTER MATTERNOT. Then convince her of this: *(Approaches IRIS and speaks to her.)* The Great Goods are

53

willing—as you might expect—to forgive you...*once.*
But after that, they may lock you up behind glass.

IRIS. Like a decoration.

MISTER MATTERNOT. Wait here. *(MATTERNOT exits.)*

MOZART. I know the feeling, Iris. Everyone just stares at
you all the time like you're perfect and you'll never
change and you'll never make a mistake—

IRIS. And everyone makes mistakes—

MOZART *(simply)*. I don't. But, I'm *afraid* I might. I'm
afraid I'll disappoint my father and never amount to anything and just be another guy in Vienna named Wolf-
gang Amadeus Mozart.

ANNABEL LEE. If you hadn't been so afraid of the water,
we'd have gotten away. There was only that ONE wave.

MOZART. But it was HUGE! Crashing and returning—over
and over again.

IRIS. And the wind was so strong—but you couldn't hear it
whistle. It was completely silent.

ANNABEL LEE. And the fog—thick as cotton—blanket-
ing the horizon in every direction. I think that fog has
captured my ship.

IRIS. I wonder when it will finally lift?

MOZART. I miss Vienna. I miss the little streets. I miss
the way my sister makes me hot cocoa. I *adore* hot cocoa, don't you?

*(LIGHTS EXPAND to reveal the Great Room of the
Great Goods. The GOODS enter, followed by MISTER
MATTERNOT and MISTER HIMTOO. GRETTA GOOD
is carrying a candelabra—with one candle, of course—
which she sets on a beautiful piano which has been
added to the room. GROTTO GOOD walks down the*

line past IRIS, MOZART and ANNABEL LEE—as though inspecting them.)

GROTTO GOOD *(with typical definitiveness).* Well, here we are—gathered and assembled and brought together here in the very midst of each other—right now, presently, at this time. Gretta?

GRETTA GOOD *(to MATTERNOT).* The shoe. *(MATTERNOT produces IRIS' tight, shiny shoe and places it on her foot during the following.)* We're glad to see it restored to your foot, Iris. And as for your clothes which became quite disheveled during your maladventure on the beach—a tailor is on his way to the island to sew you a new, best outfit. *(MATTERNOT gives IRIS a look which prompts her to say—)*

IRIS *(quietly).* Thank you.

GROTTO GOOD *(to MOZART).* You, young man, will be staying with us.

GRETTA GOOD. We've been looking for a little boy.

GROTTO GOOD. We think you'll do nicely. *(GRETTA removes the tiny piano which MOZART wears—and hands it to HIMTOO.)*

GRETTA GOOD. And you won't be needing this—

MOZART. But that's my piano—

GROTTO GOOD *(standing by the new piano in the room).* From now on—THIS is your piano.

MOZART *(excitedly, seeing the other piano).* May I play it?

GROTTO GOOD. Not now, son.

GRETTA GOOD *(to ANNABEL LEE).* And as for you, Miss Lee, the numbers are not in your favor. *(Indicating IRIS.)* For you see, we already have a girl on Great Island.

GROTTO GOOD. You're superfluous and we're sorry.

ANNABEL LEE. But I'm helping Iris find her home—

GROTTO GOOD. And you've succeeded. Now— *(He claps his hands. HIMTOO takes hold of ANNABEL LEE.)*

GRETTA GOOD. You'll be shown to the Tunnel.

GROTTO GOOD. The Tunnel of the UnWanted. *(HIMTOO begins to pull ANNABEL LEE away.)*

ANNABEL LEE. Don't worry, Iris—I'll find my ship and I'll— *(MATTERNOT steps in and stops them.)*

MISTER MATTERNOT. Is this truly necessary, Master Good?

GROTTO GOOD. Did you just *speak to me without consent?!*

MISTER MATTERNOT. My apologies, Master Good. But perhaps we can make room for another—

GROTTO GOOD. Perhaps we can make room for *you* in the *Tunnel.*

GRETTA GOOD. Off with you, now. *(MATTERNOT and HIMTOO lead ANNABEL LEE offstage. The following three speeches are spoken simultaneously.)*

ANNABEL LEE. Have courage and faith, Iris—

IRIS. Please—don't do this!

MOZART. Let her stay!

(ANNABEL LEE is gone. Smiling widely, the GOODS put their arms around IRIS and MOZART, as if posing for a quick photograph.)

GROTTO GOOD. And now here we are, a FAMILY at last! *(The clock chimes, once. The GOODS step away, admiring their children.)*

GRETTA GOOD. Do you like spaghetti?

GROTTO GOOD. We've procured the BEST noodle in all the world!

MOZART *(whispers quickly to IRIS). One* noodle?

IRIS *(whispers quickly to MOZART).* I told you.

GRETTA GOOD. What a special treat it is to welcome our new son!

GROTTO GOOD. The newest of our Goods!

GRETTA GOOD *(to MOZART).* Your father and I want you to know that you mean the world to us, and we shall provide for your every happiness here on Great Island. The tailor will measure you for your new, best clothing.

GROTTO GOOD. A perfect room shall be prepared for you.

GRETTA GOOD. And, we shall employ the best piano teacher in the world to come and give you lessons.

IRIS. Motes doesn't need a piano teacher. He's pretty good at it, already.

GRETTA GOOD. He is not a "Pretty Good." Nor are you, Iris, a "Pretty Good." We are—all of us—*Great Goods.* And that must never be forgotten!

MOZART. May I play the piano?

GROTTO GOOD. Not now, son.

MOZART. But, it's *night*—and I need to play as much as I can. The song that I'm searching for can only be captured at night. So, please, Father Good—may I play? Would that be all right? *(GROTTO looks to GRETTA. She does not have an answer. She stares right back at him. He's on his own.)*

GROTTO GOOD. Well—I'm not sure if it *is* all right—
I've never had a little boy—or a piano—so, I don't—
YES—absolutely—that would be fine—I mean—actu-
ally—in fact—NO—certainly not. Is that clear?
(MOZART just stares at him.)

IRIS. I want to see the Tunnel.

GROTTO GOOD. That's out of the question.

IRIS. Mister Matternot told us about it. He said—

GRETTA GOOD *(looking to GROTTO)*. Mister Matternot
will be reprimanded.

GROTTO GOOD. You don't want to see the Tunnel, Iris. I
assure you.

IRIS. Why not?

GROTTO GOOD. Because— *(Looking at GRETTA.)*

GRETTA GOOD. Because— *(Looking at GROTTO.)*

IRIS. Yes?

GROTTO GOOD. Because ...

GRETTA GOOD. ... you're *afraid of the Tunnel.*

IRIS. I am?

GRETTA & GROTTO GOOD. Yes. *(Silence. IRIS looks at
them, curious and hopeful.)*

IRIS. So, I've been there before?

GRETTA GOOD. Yes. *Many times*—when you were
younger.

GROTTO GOOD. And you asked us to never show it to
you again.

IRIS. I did?

GROTTO GOOD. Yes.

IRIS. Why don't I remember that? *(Silence. The GOODS
stare at her, then look away.)*

MOZART. Iris, ask them about the room.

IRIS. Did we have a white table with three chairs? And on the table was there a—

GROTTO GOOD. I think you know that *three chairs* would be out of the question.

GRETTA GOOD. Yes, now let's—

IRIS. *Tell me things.* Please. Tell me things that happened when I was little.

GRETTA GOOD. But why, Iris?

IRIS. Because I don't remember. I want you to tell me about when I was a baby. *(The GOODS look at one another.)* Please? Tell me anything—even if it's little. Tell me what my first word was. Or what my favorite toy was. Or what games we used to play. *(Silence. The GOODS stare at her. Her tone becomes more serious.)* Did we used to be happy? If we were, please tell me about that. What did that feel like? *(The GOODS stare at her for a long moment—saying nothing. Then, GROTTO turns quickly to MOZART, saying—)*

GROTTO GOOD. It's time to play the piano, son.

GRETTA GOOD. A great good idea. *(MOZART is still looking at IRIS, as GROTTO seats him at the piano bench.)*

GROTTO GOOD. You mustn't dawdle. You mustn't hesitate. You must do what you're asked when you are asked to do it. *(The GOODS prepare to listen.)*

GRETTA GOOD. Ah, the delights of a castle above us and our family around us, and now, the sweet caress of music, like water from a distant well, filling our— *(MOZART begins to play: It is, once again, the beginning of the serenade from "Eine kleine Nachtmusik." He plays it with a huge, pounding rhythm—loud and showy—but stops briefly at the end of his incomplete phrase each time ... and then immediately starts into the opening notes again, louder still, avidly searching for the song. The GOODS' reaction is horrified and immediate.)*

GROTTO GOOD. Oh, my.

GRETTA GOOD. Oh, my good.

GROTTO GOOD. Oh, good help us.

IRIS. I told you he was pretty good! *(MOZART does not hear them, does not stop playing. They step toward the piano and exclaim—)*

GRETTA GOOD. Great good son—

GROTTO & GRETTA GOOD. STOP THIS INSTANT! *(MOZART looks up at them, stops playing.)*

MOZART *(innocently).* What is it, Mother Good?

GRETTA GOOD. Grotto?

GROTTO GOOD. My son, you are now a Good. And a Good must be ... *selective.* A Good must not fritter away his time in a variety of directions. A Good must always gravitate to that which is great.

MOZART. I'll show more respect, Father Good.

GROTTO GOOD. I knew you would. *(MOZART begins to play again. He plays the identical, still incomplete passage, but this time with a languorous, melancholy feeling. Again, after a few notes, the GOODS step forward. They each take hold of one of his hands, stopping him.)*

GROTTO & GRETTA GOOD *(firmly, not with anger).* No, son. *(MOZART looks up at them, as they hold his hands.)*

IRIS. Why did you stop him? He's playing for you, he's—

GROTTO GOOD. Quiet, Iris.

GRETTA GOOD. You are very talented, my son. This talent gives you many choices.

GROTTO GOOD. And so, you must *make one.*

MOZART. Make one *what?*

GRETTA GOOD. Make one choice.

GROTTO GOOD. You must pick the Greatest Note and play *only* it. *(MOZART looks up at them. They release his hands. He looks back down at the keyboard—then back up at them.)*

MOZART. One note?

GROTTO & GRETTA GOOD. Yes.

MOZART. And *only* one? *(They nod. MOZART smiles.)* Surely you're joking!

GROTTO & GRETTA GOOD. No. *(MOZART stops smiling. The GOODS move away and prepare to listen once again. MOZART removes one of the keys—as he did earlier with his tiny piano—and holds it up, offering it.)*

MOZART. What if I gave you one and kept the rest? *(The GOODS shake their heads. MOZART returns the key to the keyboard, as the GOODS wait, expectantly.)*

GRETTA GOOD. Now, our great good son, we are ready.

MOZART. But may I say, that is not music. Music is the sound of many things coming together.

GRETTA GOOD. We await your note.

MOZART *(standing).* But there are eighty-eight keys, there are—

GROTTO GOOD. And ONE of them must be the best of all!

IRIS *(at MOZART's side).* Why? Why must everything have a "best"? With so many things in the world, it makes no sense to—

GROTTO GOOD. I warn you to say no more—

IRIS. This island is not great—it is *small.*

GRETTA GOOD. Iris!

IRIS. A "great" island would have *hundreds* of things and not just ONE!

GROTTO GOOD *(forcefully, to IRIS)*. You must be silent.

GRETTA GOOD *(forcefully, to MOZART)*. And you must choose. *(Silence. MOZART looks at them ... then sits back down at the bench, solemnly. He looks at the GOODS. They nod. Then, they close their eyes, expectantly, awaiting the playing of the "note." MOZART looks at the keyboard. His hands move—tentatively—up and down the keys ... looking for the "perfect" place to land.)*

GROTTO GOOD *(whispers)*. Oh, the expectation!

GRETTA GOOD *(whispers)*. Quiet! *(After another moment of searching, MOZART slowly lowers his finger to the keyboard and plays a note, a beautiful, low A-flat. The GOODS sigh, rapturously, and speak simultaneously.)*

GROTTO GOOD. Oh, my good...

GRETTA GOOD. Yes, that's it...

MOZART *(lifts his finger from the keyboard, looks back at the GOODS and tries to smile)*. Are you pleased?

GROTTO & GRETTA GOOD. Oh, yes.

GRETTA GOOD *(to GROTTO)*. Shall we hear it again?

GROTTO GOOD *(deliciously)*. Do you think we *dare*?

GRETTA GOOD. Yes, let's do! *(The GOODS close their eyes again and wait, expectant, as MOZART turns back to the keyboard and looks down at the "note." He pauses ... then plays the same note again. Then he plays the incomplete phrase of "Eine kleine Nachtmusik" using only the ONE note. The GOODS sigh again, audibly.)*

IRIS. Motes...

MOZART *(broken, looking down at the keys)*. It's over. I've failed. I'm never going to find that song.

(MISTER HIMTOO enters and announces—)

MISTER HIMTOO. Master Good, the tailor has arrived.

(The MEMORY MENDER enters. He does not have his cart. He has, instead, a leather case which has "Memory Mender" printed on the outside. He looks around with part dread/part curiosity—never having been to Great Island before. He does not immediately see IRIS.)

GRETTA GOOD *(approaching the MEMORY MENDER)*. We require measurements of our new son—
GROTTO GOOD *(also approaching)*. And a garment made for him that will be the finest under the—
MEMORY MENDER *(having just seen IRIS)*. Iris?
IRIS. How do you know my name?
GRETTA GOOD. Yes, that is—in fact—our daughter, Iris.
GROTTO GOOD *(a firm threat)*. And beyond saying her name—you will say *nothing more*. Do you understand? *(The MEMORY MENDER looks at them, looks at IRIS.)*
GRETTA GOOD *(coldly)*. There is a place for people who *speak more than they should*. Do you know of it? *(The MEMORY MENDER nods.)* Splendid. We have an understanding. *(GROTTO GOOD snaps his fingers, and HIMTOO brings the piano bench to center. The MEMORY MENDER gestures for MOZART to stand on the stool. During the following, the MEMORY MENDER measures MOZART with a brightly colored measuring tape.)*

IRIS. Father Good, I wonder if I could ask the tailor a question.

GROTTO GOOD *(after a look at GRETTA)*. Very well.

IRIS *(pointing to his leather case)*. What do these words mean? What is a "Memory Mender"?

MEMORY MENDER. Well, Iris, where we— *(Quickly corrects himself, looking at the GOODS.)* where *I* come from, our memories are—

GRETTA GOOD. Your memory is perfect, Iris. It holds nothing but the best of thoughts.

IRIS. Yes, but I—

GROTTO GOOD. We've arranged for you to have an unblemished past—free from sadness, free from—

IRIS. But it's not free. It's *incomplete*.

MOZART. There's a picture in her mind, and she doesn't know what it—

GROTTO GOOD. The mind plays tricks!

GRETTA GOOD. That's it!

GROTTO GOOD. Tricks and nothing more!

GRETTA GOOD *(firmly, to the MEMORY MENDER)*. *Tell her.*

MEMORY MENDER *(choosing his words carefully)*. Well—as they say—the mind can be mistaken. If one's memory is harmed—or lost—or *taken*—

GROTTO GOOD *(stepping in very close to him)*. You've said *enough*.

IRIS *(to the MEMORY MENDER)*. May I look at your buttons? *(IRIS looks at the buttons on the MEMORY MENDER's PastCoat.)* I'm looking for a girl who had a coat like yours. *(IRIS reaches into her pouch and removes the button. She hands it to the MEMORY MENDER.)* And she lost this button. Do you know where I might find her?

GROTTO GOOD. Of course he doesn't know! He's not from this island! He's a common tailor, for good's sake!

IRIS. I want him to answer me!

GRETTA GOOD. Iris—

IRIS. Why are you so afraid of him?!

GROTTO GOOD. Afraid of him?!

GRETTA GOOD. Don't be silly—

IRIS. He's a common tailor—or so you said—why won't you let him answer me? *(The GOODS look at IRIS. Then, they turn and look at the MEMORY MENDER, threateningly.)*

GRETTA GOOD *(quietly, firmly)*. He will *answer you*—

GROTTO GOOD *(quietly, firmly)*. *—carefully.* Won't you? *(The MEMORY MENDER nods. He turns to IRIS.)*

MEMORY MENDER. I know the girl of whom you speak. I made her this button myself.

IRIS. You did? *(The GOODS step in, looking at the MEMORY MENDER.)*

MEMORY MENDER *(looking into IRIS' eyes)*. But...I don't know where she is now. She should be very nearby...but I'm afraid that that girl—as I knew her—is gone. *(The GOODS smile, relieved. The MEMORY MENDER leans in more closely to IRIS and hands her the button, saying—)* I will tell you this, though: If you find her coat...you will find *her*. *(IRIS looks at him. MOZART has heard this, as well. The GOODS now begin to rush the MEMORY MENDER out of the room— with HIMTOO's help.)*

GROTTO GOOD. Is your measuring complete?

MEMORY MENDER. Well, yes, but I—

GRETTA GOOD. We expect the garment to be the best of the best.

MEMORY MENDER. Good luck, Iris—

GROTTO GOOD. Off we go, now—

IRIS. Goodbye. *(The MEMORY MENDER and HIMTOO are gone.)*

GRETTA GOOD *(happily, to MOZART)*. And now, son, before supper, why don't you play us another note?

(MOZART stares at her, as LIGHTS SHIFT to a dark, forgotten room on Great Island. All that is required is a dirty old brown table with one chair. Nearby are two other dirty chairs, lying about, broken. MISS OVER-LOOK sits at the table. She wears dark clothing, similar to MISTER MATTERNOT, MISTER OTHERGUY, etc. She is busy polishing several dark, dirty pots and pans with a wire brush. It is filthy, tedious work. MATTER-NOT enters, carrying a large box. He speaks, officiously.)

MISTER MATTERNOT. Miss Overlook, the supplies for the island have arrived from Nocturno.

MISS OVERLOOK. And the paint I requested? Did it arrive?

MISTER MATTERNOT. Your request was denied by the Goods.

MISS OVERLOOK. I only wanted to give this dark room some light.

MISTER MATTERNOT. There is, however, paint which was ordered by the Goods that—due to a flaw in its creation—will be of no use to them. It was to be thrown into the Tunnel. You're welcome to it.

MISS OVERLOOK. What flaw?

MISTER MATTERNOT. It is white. All of it. Each and every can.

MISS OVERLOOK. Why is that?

MISTER MATTERNOT. An accident in Nocturno. The Color Mixer has died. He fell from his Color Wheel during last night's storm—thrown to the ground by a great rush of wind.

MISS OVERLOOK. That's terrible.

MISTER MATTERNOT. He was given no warning. The wind, it is said, remained perfectly silent as it blew through the town. *(He sets the paint in front of her.)* You're an excellent worker, Miss Overlook. The Goods are pleased with you.

MISS OVERLOOK. I've never even met them.

MISTER MATTERNOT. That is a sign of their satisfaction. *(He starts to leave.)* Have a great good evening.

MISS OVERLOOK. Mister Matternot.

MISTER MATTERNOT. I've work of my own to do, excuse me—

MISS OVERLOOK. You once told me that I'd always lived here and always done this work. Is that true?

MISTER MATTERNOT. That is the word of the Goods.

MISS OVERLOOK. I'm not asking the Goods. I'm asking *you.* Is it true? Have I truly spent my life in this dark, musty room. Have I never seen the sky, never felt the wind?

MISTER MATTERNOT *(challenging her)*. What sky are you speaking of? What wind do you remember?

MISS OVERLOOK *(a pause as she thinks, then quietly)*. None. None at all.

MISTER MATTERNOT. Then you have your answer.

MISS OVERLOOK. But I've dreamt of such things. And
my dreams hold a picture—a picture of a family, a
house, a table set for three.

MISTER MATTERNOT. I am a worker, Miss Overlook. I
do not dote on wishes and dreams. Nor should you. Be
thankful for the *generosity* of the Goods—that they have
provided you with a room and a function. Better that
than to be thrown into the Tunnel—the home of the angry, forgotten, unremarkable things. At least you and I
are *needed* here. *(She stares at him ... and then nods.)*
You have the paint you requested. But as for seeing the
sky, don't think of it again.

*(MISTER MATTERNOT turns to leave, just as IRIS and
MOZART appear at the entrance to the room.)*

MISTER MATTERNOT. What are you doing here?

IRIS. We were just ...

MOZART. ... *looking.*

MISTER MATTERNOT. For what?

IRIS. For the way to the Tunn— *(Stops.)*

MISTER MATTERNOT. The way to the what?

MOZART. *Cocoa.* The way to the cocoa.

IRIS. Yes.

MOZART. Is it through here?

MISTER MATTERNOT. I'll have Miss Overlook find you
some cocoa.

MISS OVERLOOK. I'd be happy to.

MISTER MATTERNOT. This room is not for the children
of the Goods, it is for workers.

MISS OVERLOOK *(to IRIS).* Did you ever find your
mother? Your name is Iris, isn't it?

IRIS. Yes.

MISS OVERLOOK. I met you once. You were looking for your mother.

MISTER MATTERNOT. And she found her. The Goods are her parents. Now, it's time to—

IRIS *(opens her pouch and removes the button)*. I just remembered, you gave me this button. It had fallen off a little girl's coat. It's my oldest memory.

MISS OVERLOOK. I remember that as well. And you put the button in your pouch.

IRIS. Yes— *(MATTERNOT removes one of his gloves and reaches out his hand toward the button.)*

MISTER MATTERNOT. It's time you gave me that, Iris. It doesn't belong to you.

IRIS. But, it's my—

MISTER MATTERNOT. I'll return it for you.

IRIS. Do you know where that little girl is?

MISTER MATTERNOT. Yes, I do.

IRIS. Then, why won't you tell me?

MOZART. We needn't ask his help, Iris. If we find that coat, we'll find her. *(IRIS puts the button back in her pouch.)*

MISTER MATTERNOT. Who told you that?

MOZART. My tailor, if you must know.

MISTER MATTERNOT. Enough, now. There is to be no more discussion of coats and button and—

MISS OVERLOOK. But you were there, Mister Matternot. I remember that as well. You were there the day it happened.

MISTER MATTERNOT *(forcefully)*. Do you not know what can happen to you? *(He points in a specific direction—which IRIS and MOZART observe.)* Do you not know what awaits you in the Tunnel if you displease the Goods?!

IRIS. But she didn't—

MISTER MATTERNOT. Iris, you are *never to come to this room, again.* You don't belong here. (*Indicating OVER-LOOK.*) This woman is ordinary—just as I am—and you're not to trouble yourself with that which is ordinary. Now, return to your parents—both of you! (*IRIS and MOZART exit—but MATTERNOT does not see that they exit in the direction of the Tunnel.*) Miss Overlook, have I made myself clear?

MISS OVERLOOK. You were there. I saw you. (*As MAT-TERNOT puts his glove back on—OVERLOOK takes hold of his ungloved hand, saying.*) Your hands. There are long red scars on the palms of your hands. Why is that?

MISTER MATTERNOT. Excuse me, I need to— (*She holds tightly to his hand, not letting him leave.*)

MISS OVERLOOK. Have you always been here, as well?

MISTER MATTERNOT. Yes.

MISS OVERLOOK. And these scars on your hands. Where are they from?

MISTER MATTERNOT (*pause, simply*). I don't remember.

MISS OVERLOOK (*quietly*). It's terrible, isn't it? To forget so much. What would cause that, I wonder?

(*MUSIC PLAYS, as LIGHTS SHIFT quickly to the Tunnel. The MUSIC under the scene is joined by the SOUND of the angry, forgotten things that live in the Tunnel—the random cries of people and animals and discarded objects. The SOUND of water dripping is heard, as well. Note: A live hidden microphone causes all the following dialogue to reverberate as a slight ECHO. IRIS and MOZART are crawling on their hands and knees. IRIS has abandoned her shoe once again and is barefoot.)*

IRIS *(whispering)*. How much further?

MOZART *(also whispering)*. I wish I knew.

IRIS *(calling out)*. ANNABEL LEE! *(A frightening ECHO comes back at them—filled with the SOUND of the angry, forgotten things.)*

MOZART. What are those noises?

IRIS. The angry, forgotten things, I guess.

MOZART. I had no idea there'd be so many of them. Is that what will happen to us, someday? Discarded and forgotten—known only for the noise we once made? *(Sees something.)* Iris?

IRIS. Yes.

MOZART *(lifting it)*. Here's your other shoe. *(It is, indeed, the mate to the fancy shoe she wore earlier.)*

IRIS. I don't want it.

MOZART. No one does. *(MOZART tosses the shoe aside. As it lands, a NOISE is heard: the rolling of wheels, the clanging of metal.)* What was that?

IRIS. I think *someone's coming*— *(Another, louder noise.)*

MOZART. Or *some THING*— *(Another, still louder noise is heard.)*

IRIS. Motes, c'mon—we've got to get—

(As they start to stand and run, they immediately encounter a rusty, beat-up metal shopping cart. The cart is filled with discarded items. On the side of the shopping

*cart is a hand-lettered sign which reads: "Your Name
Here." Sitting in the shopping cart is CAPTAIN ALSO—
she wears dark, raggedy clothing with a huge number
"2" on her chest. She wears a colander as a hat and
mismatched gloves on her hands. Pushing the cart is
THIRD STRING—a man in similarly raggedy clothing
with hundreds of "Third Place" ribbons pinned to his
clothing. He wears an old football helmet with no face-
mask, and holds a single ski pole in his hand. With them is
RAY—who wears a long, dark raggedy coat, with a small,
battered black umbrella attached to his head as a hat.
He also wears dark sunglasses. Note: The effect of these
individuals is that of a strange, eccentric menace.)*

CAPTAIN ALSO. —OUT OF HERE? Is that what you
started to say? You've got to get OUT OF HERE?! Well,
fat chance there is of THAT. You're DOWN UNDER, now.
You're in the middle of the mediocre middle. *(IRIS and
MOZART try to turn and run the other way—but RAY
intercepts them and blocks their way.)* And now that
you're here, you've got to answer to ME.

IRIS. Who are you?

CAPTAIN ALSO. I'm Captain Also, the Dean of the Dis-
cards, the Chairman of the Abhorred. I'm second best to
all the rest. And this is Third String—

THIRD STRING *(menacingly)*. Have a nice *grey*.

CAPTAIN ALSO. Third String is not a winner and he's not
a loser. He is undeniably *average*. So, I made him my
CEO.

THIRD STRING. Chief *Extra* Officer.

CAPTAIN ALSO. We are the Top of what's on the Bottom, the most Famous of the Forgotten! *(CAPTAIN*

ALSO reaches into the shopping cart and pulls out some items, tossing them at IRIS and MOZART.) You want a TOASTER?—we got millions of 'em. HANGERS—PLAS-TIC TUBS—BRIDESMAID DRESSES—we got *millions of 'em.* Everybody wanted 'em ONCE—

THIRD STRING. —and nobody wants 'em NOW.

CAPTAIN ALSO. We are the Orphans of the Ordinary!

THIRD STRING. Unexceptional—

CAPTAIN ALSO. —and Unnecessary!

MOZART. And who's that?

THIRD STRING. That's Ray.

IRIS. Is he ordinary, too?

CAPTAIN ALSO. No, he's displaced. Ray used to work for the Sun. He did outreach. Show 'em, Ray— *(RAY opens his coat to reveal its brilliantly yellow lining.)* You ever wonder what happens to the Sun when you shade your eyes, or step under a tree to cool off? Ever wonder where those Rays of Sun end up once they're not needed anymore? *(RAY closes his coat.)* You got it. They end up right here. Just like the two of you.

THIRD STRING. What's your business here? Who threw *you* out?

IRIS. Nobody threw us out.

CAPTAIN ALSO. What?!

THIRD STRING. Then what are you doing in the Tunnel?!

MOZART. We're searching for our friend.

RAY. "Friend"—what's that? Won't find any of those down here.

IRIS. Why not?

RAY. If you're a friend—somebody wants you. There's no one like that down here.

MOZART. You see, we were living with the Goods, but we—

CAPTAIN ALSO. The GOODS?! We've got a couple of GOODS here?! Get 'em! *(THIRD STRING surprises IRIS and MOZART from behind, putting his ski pole under their chins—trapping them in place. RAY moves in on them, as well.)* Oh, we've been waiting for this moment. Haven't we, Ray?

RAY. Since the day they turned me into shade.

CAPTAIN ALSO. And we're not alone. Do you hear them? *(The SOUND of the angry forgotten things begins to grow louder and louder.)* Do you hear all the angry, forgotten things? They've been waiting for you and now they'll have their revenge! *(CAPTAIN ALSO gestures, quickly and dramatically, and the SOUND of the angry forgotten things stops, instantly.)*

THIRD STRING. Tell us your story, so we can devise your punishment.

CAPTAIN ALSO. Yeah—tell us what makes you SPECIAL. *(To MOZART.)* You first.

MOZART. Me? Oh, nothing, really. Nothing in the least.

THIRD STRING. C'mon. You're a Good. Spill the beans.

MOZART. I've just written a few songs.

THIRD STRING. A few?

MOZART. Well, ten sonatas and three symphonies by the age of nine—

CAPTAIN ALSO. I see.

MOZART. But there's a song—or part of a song—that I'm still looking for.

RAY. You won't find it here. People *want* music—so, there's no music down here.

THIRD STRING *(to IRIS)*. And what about you?

CAPTAIN ALSO. Yeah—what's your *story*?

IRIS. I don't have one.

THIRD STRING. Sure you do. Everybody's got a story. Even Ray.

RAY. It all started on a sunny day in a—

CAPTAIN ALSO & THIRD STRING. Shut up, Ray.

IRIS. I wish I had one. But, I don't.

THIRD STRING. She's lying.

IRIS. All I have is a picture in my mind.

CAPTAIN ALSO. A picture of when you were *wanted?* A picture of your *home?*

IRIS. Yes, I think so—

CAPTAIN ALSO. Well, FORGET ABOUT IT. Because you'll never get back to it.

THIRD STRING. Nobody ever leaves the Tunnel.

MOZART. But, why?

CAPTAIN ALSO. Because *the only way out of here is to be* WANTED—

THIRD STRING. To be USEFUL—

RAY. So, we're TRAPPED—

CAPTAIN ALSO. Just like *you.*

(They tighten their grips on IRIS and MOZART, as ANNABEL LEE enters, holding a wooden ship's wheel in her hand. Strapped over her shoulder is what appears to be a large, fabric satchel of some kind. She goes directly to CAPTAIN ALSO, THIRD STRING and RAY.)

ANNABEL LEE. Unhand them this instant and prepare to set sail!

MOZART *(simultaneously)*. Annabel Lee!

IRIS *(simultaneously)*. There she is!

CAPTAIN ALSO. You know her?

ANNABEL LEE. There's a speedy escape should you do
   what I say—
       Or a watery grave should you me disobey.

RAY. Who are you?

ANNABEL LEE. When the fog is lifted and the tide is high—
       We will sail our ship and bid the Goods goodbye!

THIRD STRING. Ship? What ship?

ANNABEL LEE. Now, unhand them and see to your duties!

CAPTAIN ALSO. We don't answer to you, Miss Whoever-
   YouAre. These Goods are our prisoners here, and—

ANNABEL LEE. And I am your *captain. (She tosses the
   ship's wheel to CAPTAIN ALSO—who catches it and
   holds it, proudly. Silence, then—)*

THIRD STRING. You mean...

CAPTAIN ALSO. ...you *need us?*

ANNABEL LEE. I can't sail without you.

THIRD STRING. You mean...

RAY. ...you'll *free us from the Tunnel?*

ANNABEL LEE. If you'll unhand my friends and serve as
   my crew—
       Your discarded days will vanish from view.
   *(CAPTAIN ALSO, THIRD STRING and RAY release
   their grip on IRIS and MOZART.)* Now, fall in. *(THIRD
   STRING and RAY line up next to CAPTAIN ALSO's
   shopping cart—forming a line. ANNABEL LEE walks
   past them, taking stock of her new crew.)* The ship
   waits—trapped in fog—at the far end of this Tunnel.
   There are sails to mend, rigging to ready, and provisions
   to load.
       Are you able, willing and sufficiently brave—
       To conquer the sea and make fear your slave?

STILL LIFE WITH IRIS

CAPTAIN ALSO, THIRD STRING, RAY *(saluting)*. We are!

ANNABEL LEE. Now, to the ship! *(ANNABEL LEE gestures off, and the three of them rush off, pushing CAPTAIN ALSO who steers with the ship's wheel. IRIS and MOZART approach ANNABEL LEE.)*

IRIS. How did you find the ship in all that fog?

ANNABEL LEE. I was looking for parts of your picture— the table, the flower, the vase. So, I kept following the Tunnel, on and on. And I saw something shining in the distance—a shimmering patch of light—and when I reached it— *(She removes the satchel from over her shoulder—and we see that it is actually a faded and weathered PastCoat which she has used to carry an object. She unwraps the object. It is a vase—identical to that in the "Still Life.")* I found vases. Hundreds of them. Discarded in a huge pile. *(ANNABEL LEE hands the vase to IRIS.)*

IRIS. Just like the picture in my mind.

ANNABEL LEE. And there the Tunnel empties into a cove, shrouded in fog. And when I lifted this vase, the light cut through the fog and there it was … my ship, awaiting me. *(IRIS has discovered the weathered PastCoat.)*

IRIS. Motes, look.

MOZART. Is that the coat you're looking for? Is it missing a button?

IRIS *(looking closely at the coat)*. No. And it's too big to be a little girl's.

ANNABEL LEE. There are hundreds of those coats, piled up at the far end of the Tunnel.

IRIS. We'll need to get all of them. *(To ANNABEL LEE.)* Can you make it back there?

ANNABEL LEE *(nods).* I found a shortcut through the water.

IRIS. Good. And take Motes with you. *(IRIS takes the vase and rewraps it in the old PastCoat.)*

MOZART *(to ANNABEL LEE).* Wait ... did you say *water?*

ANNABEL LEE *(tossing him a discarded life preserver).* It's an easy swim. There's only that ONE wave—

MOZART. I would like to rethink our entire plan—

(ANNABEL LEE ushers MOZART off, and IRIS exits, opposite, as LIGHTS SHIFT to Miss Overlook's room. The table is now white. One of the chairs is painted white. Another is half-painted. The third remains a dirty brown. An open can of paint sits nearby. MISS OVER-LOOK enters and sets a steaming cup of cocoa on the table in front of the one painted chair. She looks down at the table for a moment, touching the back of the white chair, as IRIS enters, carrying the wrapped vase.)

IRIS. Miss Overlook—

MISS OVERLOOK. Is Mozart with you? I have his cocoa for him.

IRIS. He'll be here. I wanted to ask you something.

MISS OVERLOOK. What do you have there? *(IRIS un-wraps the vase and sets it on the table—however, her focus is clearly on the PastCoat.)*

IRIS. It's something we found in the Tunnel. Would you hold on to it for me?

MISS OVERLOOK. By all means.

IRIS. What I wanted to ask you about was *this*. *(IRIS holds up the PastCoat, showing it to OVERLOOK.)* Have you ever seen this before? *(Silence, as OVERLOOK looks at the coat.)*

MISS OVERLOOK. Not that coat, Iris. But one like it. On the day I met you.

IRIS. Yes, I remember that as well. It belonged to a little girl.

MISS OVERLOOK. It belonged to you. *(Pause.)* You had a coat like this.

IRIS. What happened to it?

MISS OVERLOOK. It's better that you don't know, Iris. That's what Mister Matternot said and I see now that he was right.

IRIS. But why would he say that?

MISS OVERLOOK. He took your coat from you. I watched him as he did it. *(Pause.)* At the time, I thought he was very kind. For before he took your coat, you were very upset—you were calling for your mother.

IRIS. My mother?

MISS OVERLOOK. Yes. But then, a moment later, he took your coat from you...and you were fine. *(Pause.)* He did it to protect you.

IRIS. I don't want that. Not anymore. *(IRIS stares at her— then rushes out of the room, taking the coat with her.)*

MISS OVERLOOK. Iris—!

(As LIGHTS SHIFT quickly to the Great Room, MISTER OTHERGUY and MISTER HIMTOO are putting a large, ornate glass case in place. It is an exact replica of the small case which held Iris' doll—including the lock on

*one side of it. MISTER MATTERNOT enters, watching,
as GRETTA and GROTTO GOOD enter, opposite.)*

MISTER MATTERNOT. Master Good, if I may ask, what
is the meaning of this?

GROTTO GOOD. You may not ask. You may not ask it at
all.

GRETTA GOOD. You were given a task, Matternot. You
were told to bring us a little girl and make certain that
she felt at home.

GROTTO GOOD. You were to remove any vestige of her
past.

MISTER MATTERNOT. And that's what I did!

GROTTO GOOD. To the contrary—this girl, Iris, has
grown curious about her Before-Good life.

GRETTA GOOD. You have displeased us—

GROTTO GOOD. —And we have your Fate under consid-
eration.

MISTER MATTERNOT. And Iris—what of her? You
can't hope to keep her here. Now that she is curious, she
will—

GROTTO GOOD. It's no longer your concern.

GRETTA GOOD. We've found a fine place for her.

GROTTO GOOD. A fitting home for the greatest of our
Goods!

*(The GOODS start off, as IRIS enters—carrying the old,
tattered PastCoat—and goes directly to MISTER MAT-
TERNOT. Seeing IRIS, the GOODS stop at a distance,
listening. MISTER OTHERGUY and MISTER HIMTOO
stand on either side of the glass case.)*

IRIS. Mister Matternot—

MISTER MATTERNOT *(seeing the coat in her hand)*. Iris, what do you have in your—

IRIS. The coat you showed me. It was *mine*, wasn't it? Tell me the truth. It was mine and you took it from me.

MISTER MATTERNOT. You had been *chosen*, Iris. The Great Goods had—

IRIS. You lied to me—

MISTER MATTERNOT. I was trying to save you—

IRIS. Save me?

MISTER MATTERNOT. From your sadness. From the loss of your home. Believe me, it was the only way I could—

IRIS. But why would you take my coat?

MISTER MATTERNOT. It holds your *past*, Iris—it holds the story of your life.

GROTTO GOOD *(stepping in)*. Matternot—!

IRIS. Take me back there.

MISTER MATTERNOT. I can't—

IRIS. Take me back to that room—

MISTER MATTERNOT. That room is gone. *(Forcefully.)* Just like your mother. It is gone and you must forget about it.

IRIS. Who was she? *Tell me. (The GOODS approach IRIS.)*

GRETTA GOOD. Your life is here with us, Iris.

GROTTO GOOD. We've given you the BEST things in all the world—

IRIS. You've given me everything but the thing I want most: *the story of who I am.* Even the common, forgotten things know where they came from—but I don't. I wish I was one of them.

GRETTA GOOD *(simultaneously)*. Don't say that—
GROTTO GOOD *(simultaneously)*. Iris, that's enough—

IRIS *(to MATTERNOT, desperately)*. *I want you to take me
to that room!*

MISTER MATTERNOT *(simultaneously)*. But, Iris, I—
GRETTA GOOD. *(simultaneously)*. Put it out of your mind.

GROTTO GOOD. We have a greater place for you, Iris!
    *(GROTTO and GRETTA clap their hands, and OTHER-
    GUY and HIMTOO step forward and grab IRIS. The
    old, tattered PastCoat falls to the ground.)*
MISTER MATTERNOT. What are you doing?
IRIS. Let go of me—
GRETTA GOOD. You will be the glory of Great Island!
    *(MUSIC, as MATTERNOT runs toward IRIS, but is re-
    strained by OTHERGUY, as HIMTOO takes IRIS to the
    glass case. The GOODS remove the lock and open the
    door to the case.)*
MISTER MATTERNOT. You can't do this. You must tell
    her—you must tell her the truth!
GRETTA GOOD. Had you done your job well, this could
    have been avoided—
IRIS *(cries out)*. No—please don't do this—
GRETTA GOOD. But now she must pay for your mis-
    takes—
MISTER MATTERNOT. No, listen to me—
GROTTO GOOD. Her pain is your doing, Matternot. Her
    sadness is your curse. *(IRIS is placed inside the glass
    case. The lock is attached by GROTTO—who holds the
    large key ring with the one key aloft, proudly. IRIS*

stands, trying to plead with the GOODS through the glass, "Why are you doing this?" "Please, don't leave me in here!" etc., but she cannot be heard. The GOODS exit, followed by OTHERGUY and HIMTOO. IRIS stares out, helplessly, as MATTERNOT tries to talk to her through the glass.)

MISTER MATTERNOT *(painfully, from his heart)*. I was afraid, Iris—afraid of the wrath of the Goods—that they'd send me to the Tunnel and I would die alone and forgotten. But worse than the Tunnel is what I've done to you; given you glimpses of your home and nothing more. *(Pause.)* What our memory leaves unfinished, our heart completes with ache. *(MATTERNOT puts his ungloved hand up and presses it against the glass. IRIS looks at him—then matches his gesture with her hand.)* Forgive me, Iris.

(ANNABEL LEE and MOZART rush on. MOZART carries a huge bundle of PastCoats in his arms.)

ANNABEL LEE. What have you done with her?!

MISTER MATTERNOT. I was trying to—

MOZART *(dropping the coats to the ground)*. You've locked her up behind glass.

MISTER MATTERNOT. No, it was the Goods who—

(The GOODS rush on, followed by MISTER OTHERGUY and MISTER HIMTOO.)

GRETTA GOOD. What is all the motion and commotion?!

GROTTO GOOD *(seeing ANNABEL LEE)*. And what are you doing here?! You were discarded!

ANNABEL LEE. Well, I'm *back. (MATTERNOT is now standing near the pile of PastCoats.)*

MISTER MATTERNOT *(forcefully, to the GOODS).* Now I see what you've done! *(He kneels amid the coats, lifting armfuls of them as he speaks.)* All these years— I had no idea!

GROTTO GOOD *(simultaneously).* What is that?

GRETTA GOOD *(simultaneously).* What's there?

MISTER MATTERNOT. *Coats.* Look at all of them!

GRETTA GOOD. We've given each of them a Great Good life.

MISTER MATTERNOT. You told me there were only *two.* Only Iris and her mother. But there have been HUNDREDS!

GROTTO GOOD. Not another word, Matternot—

MISTER MATTERNOT *(referring to HIMTOO and OTHER-GUY).* You've done this to *all of us,* haven't you?!

GROTTO GOOD *(throwing the key ring to OTHERGUY).* Lock him away as well! *(As OTHERGUY catches the key ring and starts toward MATTERNOT, MATTERNOT throws one of the PastCoats from the pile to OTHER-GUY, saying—)*

MISTER MATTERNOT. You've ripped the past from each and every one of us! *(Upon catching the coat, OTHER-GUY stops. He looks down at the coat, holding it tightly in one hand, the key ring in the other, then he looks at the GOODS—puzzled, wanting an answer.)*

GRETTA GOOD. You've been given an order, Mister Otherguy—

MISTER MATTERNOT *(to OTHERGUY).* That's not your name. Your name was stolen from you by the Goods—

GROTTO GOOD. Mister Himtoo—take that coat from him! (*As HIMTOO rushes at OTHERGUY, MATTERNOT throws a coat from the pile to HIMTOO—who, upon catching it, immediately stops. He, too, looks at the coat, then up at the GOODS—puzzled, wanting an answer.*)

MISTER MATTERNOT. It's too late—now they know the truth. (*OTHERGUY and HIMTOO look at their coats, at each other. Then they put their coats on and approach the GOODS with menace.*)

GROTTO GOOD. This, Gretta, is a great good problem. (*MATTERNOT lifts the pile of PastCoats from the ground—inadvertently leaving behind the single, tattered PastCoat which is laying elsewhere—and rushes off, saying—*)

MISTER MATTERNOT. Soon everyone will know!

GROTTO GOOD (*simultaneously*). NO—
GRETTA GOOD (*simultaneously*). MATTERNOT—

(*The GOODS start to rush off after MATTERNOT—but are stopped by OTHERGUY and HIMTOO. ANNABEL LEE takes the key from OTHERGUY and opens the glass case, freeing IRIS, saying—*)

ANNABEL LEE. Don't worry, Iris. My ship is rigged and ready—

MOZART. And her crew is second to none—

ANNABEL LEE. And the moment the fog is lifted, we shall sail away and be gone.

IRIS. Thank you both. (*OTHERGUY and HIMTOO begin to place the GOODS inside the glass case.*)

GROTTO GOOD (to OTHERGUY and HIMTOO). You wouldn't dare!

GRETTA GOOD. Grotto, dear, what will become of us?! (ANNABEL LEE tosses the key back to OTHERGUY— and the GOODS are locked inside, silently pleading for help.)

MOZART. Now, let's get off this island before being a Good gets any worse. (ANNABEL LEE sees the tattered PastCoat which was left behind. She lifts it.)

ANNABEL LEE. Mister Matternot left this behind—the old and tattered one.

IRIS (taking it from her). I'll bring it with me. C'mon—

(IRIS rushes off, followed by ANNABEL LEE and MOZART, as the MUSIC CHANGES to that of the "Still Life," and LIGHTS SHIFT to Miss Overlook's room. MISS OVERLOOK holds a paintbrush in her hand, making a few final brush strokes on the third and final white chair. The table and chairs in the room are now all painted white. She positions the vase in the center of the table. She moves the cocoa slightly—so that it is now in the exact position seen in the "Still Life." The "Still Life" is now lacking only the iris. OVERLOOK takes a long look at the table, then exits—exactly as she did in Act One, as MISTER MATTERNOT enters, opposite. He now carries only one PastCoat in his arms. He stops when he sees the white table and vase.)

MISTER MATTERNOT. Miss Overlook? (No response. MATTERNOT takes a long look at the table, then he lowers the coat, revealing something he is holding in his hands...it is an iris. He places the iris in the vase. The

"Still Life" is now complete. MUSIC CONTINUES as MATTERNOT steps away from the table, and IRIS enters, carrying the old, tattered PastCoat. IRIS stops when she sees the "Still Life." She steps towards the table. Walks around it, slowly. IRIS takes the button from her pouch. She closes her eyes and rubs it in her hand, as the LIGHT on the table grows brighter and brighter. She opens her eyes and compares the picture in her mind with the picture in front of her. They are identical. The MUSIC FADES away.)

IRIS *(quietly)*. That's it.

(IRIS moves to the table. She pulls "her" chair back from the table—exactly as she did in Act One. She sits. She looks at the vase, the flower, the cocoa in front of her. Then—just as she did in Act One—she begins to reach for the cocoa, as MISS OVERLOOK enters.)

MISS OVERLOOK *(simply)*. Careful. That's hot.

IRIS *(looks at her. Then, simply, quietly)*. Mom.

MISS OVERLOOK. Yes, I know, Iris. I know you miss her. Whoever she is, wherever she's gone. *(MATTERNOT takes the PastCoat and walks towards OVERLOOK. She looks at him, puzzled.)* Mister Matternot?

MISTER MATTERNOT. I'd like you to meet someone. *(MATTERNOT helps OVERLOOK put on the coat—her PastCoat. When it is on, she looks first at the table ... and then at IRIS.)*

MOM [formerly MISS OVERLOOK] *(quietly)*. Iris. *(IRIS and MOM embrace.)* Oh, Iris, I'm right here. And now wherever you are, no matter how far away—

IRIS. —when you call my name, I'll hear you.

MOM. Thank you, Mister Matternot. *(MOM turns and looks at MATTERNOT. Then, she approaches him.)* I'd like to see your hands, if I could. *(MOM helps MATTERNOT remove his gloves. He stares at her, puzzled. MOM hands the gloves to IRIS. IRIS takes them, confused.)* Here, Iris. These gloves belong in your pouch. *(MOM touches the palms of MATTERNOT's hands as she looks into his eyes, speaking softly.)* These scars on your hands. They belong to the man who roped the moon every night, and hauled it down out of the sky. And then he'd give the signal for the sun to rise...

IRIS *(looking at MATTERNOT)*. ...and the day to break. *(MOM holds out her hand, and IRIS hands her the tattered PastCoat. MOM helps MATTERNOT put his Past-Coat on.)*

MOM. Do you remember us?

DAD [formerly MISTER MATTERNOT] *(quietly)*. Yes.

MOM. Even with your coat tattered and torn?

DAD. Your name is Rose.

MOM. Yes. *(Pause.)* And this is your daughter, Iris. *(IRIS and DAD stare at each other.)*

IRIS. I thought you left us.

DAD. The Great Goods took me away, Iris. Just like you.

IRIS. Do you remember me?

DAD. You were just a baby. And my coat is old and worn—

IRIS. Don't worry, Dad—we'll be your coat. We'll tell you everything you missed.

(DAD and IRIS embrace, as ANNABEL LEE and MOZART enter. ANNABEL LEE is carrying a smaller PastCoat in her arms.)

MOZART. The coats have all been returned, Iris.

ANNABEL LEE. We've given everyone back their Pasts.

MOM. And what of the Goods?

DAD. The Goods reign is over. They work for *us* now.

ANNABEL LEE. They're loading Motes' piano onto my ship.

MOZART *(deliciously). One note at a time.*

ANNABEL LEE *(holding up the coat).* There's one coat left, Iris. *(DAD takes the coat from ANNABEL LEE. MOM and DAD put the PastCoat on IRIS, and then stand, holding each other, arm in arm.)*

IRIS. Thank you. *(Turning to ANNABEL LEE and MOZART.)* I hope you find your song, Motes.

MOZART. I'll try again tonight. Perhaps I'll find it just before the sun rises.

IRIS *(giving ANNABEL LEE the button).* Annabel Lee, this is for you.

ANNABEL LEE. But this button—it's part of your coat—

IRIS. And now I'm part of yours. *(ANNABEL LEE smiles.)* I'll lift the fog for you as soon as I get home. *(ANNABEL LEE and IRIS embrace.)*

MOZART. Hey, Iris—

IRIS. What?

MOZART. Are you going to drink that cocoa?

IRIS *(smiles and hands the cup of cocoa to MOZART).* Take it with you, Motes. *(ANNABEL LEE and MOZART leave, saying—)*

ANNABEL LEE *(simultaneously).* Good sailing, Iris!

MOZART *(simultaneously).* Adieu!

(IRIS looks at her MOM and DAD—who have taken their places at the table. IRIS joins them.)

IRIS. But how will *we* get home?

DAD *(simply)*. By *remembering*.

MOM *(quietly)*. What do you see, Iris?

IRIS *(slowly, quietly)*. I see an iris in a vase. And the vase is on a table. And the table is in a house. And the house is—

(A flourish of MUSIC, as LIGHTS REVEAL the Land of Nocturno, once again—identical to the beginning of the play. The "WELCOME TO NOCTURNO" sign is there. The rain barrel is there—marked with the number of a new batch. And, approaching the table from a distance are HAZEL and ELMER—each holding a still-spotless Ladybug; and the FLOWER PAINTER—painting a rose.)

IRIS *(opens her eyes)*. —in Nocturno, our home!

ELMER *(simultaneously)*. Hazel, look—

HAZEL *(simultaneously)*. Iris!

FLOWER PAINTER *(simultaneously)*. Here they are!

(IRIS, MOM and DAD step away from the table.)

IRIS. Does it look the same to you, Dad?

DAD *(looking around)*. Some of it does... *(The FLOWER PAINTER gives the rose to MOM, as HAZEL and ELMER approach IRIS.)*

FLOWER PAINTER. Welcome home, Rose. The wind's been silent without you.

MOM *(smiles)*. You'll hear it again in no time.

HAZEL *(to IRIS, like she never left)*. Did you find the spots, Iris?

IRIS. The what?

ELMER (*holding up his Ladybug*). For the Ladybugs? (*IRIS reaches into her PastCoat and removes one large, black spot. She hands it to ELMER.*)
IRIS. Where I was, Elmer, they only had *one*.

(*HAZEL smiles and embraces IRIS, as ELMER looks puzzled, and the MEMORY MENDER pushes his cart into the midst of the celebration, cranky as ever.*)

MEMORY MENDER. Well, look at this, a bunch a people huggin' and pattin' each other on their coats—when they oughta be takin' care of each sleeve and button and—
DAD (*approaches the MEMORY MENDER; with a smile of recognition*). Well, one thing in Nocturno hasn't changed. You're still as cranky as ever! (*A pause, while the MEMORY MENDER stares at DAD, trying hard to place him in his memory. The others look on. The MEMORY MENDER looks hard at DAD—while at the same time touching various parts of his own coat, saying—*)
MEMORY MENDER. Wait—wait—wait—don't tell me— (*After a few tries, the MEMORY MENDER touches a small button at the end of his sleeve, saying—*) The Day Breaker! Husband of Rose, father of Iris.
DAD (*shaking his hand*). That's me.
MEMORY MENDER. I gotta tighten that button down before I *lose you completely*. (*To IRIS.*) I see you found your coat, Iris. Welcome home.
IRIS. Thank you.
MEMORY MENDER (*to DAD*). And you know, I had to rope the moon for you every night while you've been gone. It's awful hard on the hands—
DAD. Yes, it is.

MEMORY MENDER. In fact, I just now put her away for the day.

DAD. Have you given the sun her signal to rise?

MEMORY MENDER. Have at it. I got coats to sew. *(He moves away, still talking.)* People 'round here think the past's just some kind of toy that their mind plays with, but you gotta take care of it or you'll trip and get a rip— *(The MEMORY MENDER moves upstage and looks on as he sews. The others turn and look at DAD.)*

DAD *(turning to IRIS and her MOM)*. Ready? *(From a great distance ... MUSIC PLAYS the first few phases of the Serenade in G from "Eine kleine Nachtmusik," as before. DAD reaches out his arm in front of him—preparing to raise it, as IRIS steps in, interrupting him.)*

IRIS. Wait, Dad. Wait one ... more ... moment. *(As soon as IRIS has said this, the full Mozart serenade continues and plays on—uninterrupted—for the first time. IRIS nods to her DAD, smiling. EVERYONE looks out at the horizon. IRIS stands next to her DAD, as he reaches his arm out in front of him, preparing to give the sun its "signal," preparing to break the new day.)* Almost day.

DAD. Almost day, indeed. *(DAD lifts his arm, dramatically, in front of him, as upstage, a huge sun lifts into place and a brilliant orange glow illuminates all of them. The MUSIC BUILDS and fills the theatre as the people of Nocturno gradually return to their work, except for IRIS, who stands front, home at last, looking up into the glorious morning light, as the LIGHTS FADE to black.)*

END OF PLAY

PRODUCTION NOTES

SETTING –

The Land of Nocturno
A fantastical world, whose inhabitants spend each night readying the "known" world for the next day. This is not, however, a land of night and darkness. Quite the opposite. It is a land of color and pragmatic magic. It exists in a world parallel to our own.

Great Island
A magnificent and remote inland isle. This is the home of the Great Goods, the rulers of the people of Nocturno.

The Great Room of the Great Goods
The feel of this room is quite the opposite of a home—more like that of a museum. Many of the objects are housed in glass cases and cordoned off with velvet ropes. These include: one gargoyle—though there is obviously a place for its missing mate—sitting near the one door; one window with a curtain on only one side of it; one bookcase which holds one book—propped up with one bookend; one chair; one table with one goblet on it; one lamp; one very large plant containing only one large leaf; one framed fish; and one mounted elk's head, with only one set of antlers. There is a large clock, with only the number 1 on its face, and sitting prominently in the room is an ornate toy box.

The Tunnel
This is an ominous stretch of the stage defined almost exclusively by lighting. Perhaps a series of tattered, low-

hanging pieces of fabric—splattered with odd graffiti—to
create the necessary sense of claustrophobia.

PASTCOATS –

All of the inhabitants of Nocturno wear long, brightly colored coats, decorated—perhaps—with a variety of small
cloth patches, beads or other mementos. Each coat contains
the *past* of the person wearing it—and is known, therefore,
as a "PastCoat."

MUSIC –

The music of Mozart—in all its richness, variance and
breadth—underscores the play.

TRANSITIONS –

The first line of every scene is intended to immediately follow the last line of the previous scene. This obviously requires a playing space that can quickly and *simply* represent
a variety of locales. This also means that the first line of
any scene can be played as an "entrance" by the speaking
character.

APPENDIX

Note on Magic Designed for this Play

For the Childsplay (Arizona) production of STILL LIFE WITH IRIS, illusionist Steffan Soule designed and incorporated a variety of simple, wonderful, character-based magic effects which were performed by the cast. These included a "flower painting" illusion for the Flower Painter, a "fog lifter" illusion for Iris, a "lightning bolt" illusion for the Bolt Bender, a "thimble" illusion for the Memory Mender, and a "candle" illusion for Mister Himtoo, among others.

To obtain more information about licensing and performing these and other magic effects designed specifically for this play, please contact:

Steffan Soule / A Touch of Magic
2452 60th Ave. SE
Mercer Island WA 98040
(206) 232-9129

Alternate Version of this Play – Featuring Major Stage Illusions

The premiere production of STILL LIFE WITH IRIS featured not only some of the smaller magic effects listed above but also three major stage illusions created by Steffan Soule and Cooper Edens. The script for this alternate version of the play is available through Dramatic Publishing. However, all inquires regarding the use of these copyrighted, one-of-a-kind illusions must be directed to Steffan Soule, at the address listed above.

Following is a brief description of each major illusion and its use in the story of the play:

GIANT TOY BLOCKS

This illusion replaces the toy box which Iris is given on page 41. The Goods present Iris with a giant puzzle made up of enormous toy blocks. With help from Mister Matternot, Mister Otherguy and Mister Himtoo, Iris stacks the giant blocks in such a way that they form a picture ... a picture of Nocturno, her home. When Iris hears the Goods returning, she magically enters the picture—as the flat surface of the solid blocks mysteriously becomes three-dimensional. The Goods arrive and see Iris standing "inside" the world of the blocks. As they try to go after her, the blocks become solid once again. The Goods and their workers dismantle the stack of blocks ... but Iris has vanished.

SEASHELLS

This illusion replaces the seashell or stone mentioned on page 42. Iris finds two enormous seashells on the shore of Great Island. She calls out ... and her voice echoes back to her from one of the empty shells. Iris opens a special door in the shell ... revealing Annabel Lee.

As Iris and Annabel Lee sing "Twinkle Twinkle Little Star," Mozart appears from out of the second shell, playing the song on his tiny piano.

When the storm comes, Mozart and Annabel Lee seek shelter inside their respective shells. When Iris opens the doors of the shells ... her two friends have magically switched places.

When Mister Matternot and Mister Otherguy are heard approaching, Iris climbs inside one of the shells to hide; Annabel Lee and Mozart disappear into the other one. When Matternot and Otherguy are gone, Iris emerges from her shell and opens the other shell ... but Annabel Lee and

Mozart have <u>vanished</u>. A moment later, they <u>magically appear</u> out in the audience, beckoning Iris to join them.

HOURGLASS

This illusion replaces the glass case on page 79. A giant hourglass is rolled onstage. The Goods, to keep Iris from running away, lock her in the top portion of the hourglass. The bottom portion of it is filled with sand.

When alone with Mister Matternot, Iris insists he turn the giant lever on the side of the hourglass. She thinks this may be a way to free herself. Matternot turns the lever... the hourglass tilts and turns over... and the sand runs through the glass, completely burying Iris.

The Goods, Annabel Lee and Mozart enter and turn the lever once again. When the hourglass turns over and the sand runs through again... Iris has completely <u>vanished</u>.

The Goods rush off. Annabel Lee and Mozart turn the lever again... and Iris <u>magically appears</u>, once again, in the top of the hourglass. The three of them escape.

The Goods reappear and turn the lever one more time. The hourglass turns over and the sand runs through... revealing <u>Mister Himtoo</u> trapped inside the glass.

97

WHAT PEOPLE ARE SAYING about *Still Life with Iris* ...

"Wonderful! One of the most clever, profound plays for children I've ever read, with enough character complexity to impress even adult professional actors."
Luann Purcell,
First Stage, Atlanta, Ga.

"*Still Life with Iris* deserves the prizes it has won. It raises much more significant issues—the importance of history, the dangers of perfectionism, how to parent—than most plays for young audiences, yet is fast-paced, fun and visual."
Karen Bovard,
Watkinson School, Hartford, Conn.

"The actors' perception of their world within and without the play was deepened and enjoyed more for doing this wonderful play. We all felt it was the best show we've ever done for the 7th and 8th-grade drama classes."
Linda Khoury,
Hammond School, Columbia, S.C.

DIRECTOR'S NOTES

DIRECTOR'S NOTES

DIRECTOR'S NOTES

DIRECTOR'S NOTES

DIRECTOR'S NOTES

DIRECTOR'S NOTES